How to make
$40,000 A YEAR
with your
WOODWORKING

How to make
$40,000 A YEAR
with your
WOODWORKING

Sal Maccarone

POPULAR WOODWORKING BOOKS
CINCINNATI, OH

READ THIS IMPORTANT SAFETY NOTICE

To prevent accidents, keep safety in mind while you work. Use the safety guards installed on power equipment; they are for your protection. When working on power equipment, keep fingers away from saw blades, wear safety goggles to prevent injuries from flying wood chips and sawdust, wear headphones to protect your hearing, and consider installing a dust vacuum to reduce the amount of airborne sawdust in your woodshop. Don't wear loose clothing, such as neckties or shirts with loose sleeves, or jewelry, such as rings, necklaces or bracelets, when working on power equipment, and tie back long hair to prevent it from getting caught in your equipment. The author and editors who compiled this book have tried to make the contents as accurate and correct as possible. Plans, illustrations, photographs and text have been carefully checked. All instructions, plans and projects should be carefully read, studied and understood before beginning construction. Due to the variability of local conditions, construction materials, skill levels, etc., neither the author nor Popular Woodworking Books assumes any responsibility for any accidents, injuries, damages or other losses incurred resulting from the material presented in this book.

Library of Congress Cataloging-in-Publication Data

Maccarone, Sal.
    How to make $40,000 a year with your woodworking / Sal Maccarone.
      p.   cm.
    Includes index.
    ISBN 1-55870-480-9 (pbk.)
    1. Woodworking industries—Management. 2. New business enterprises—Management. 3. Woodwork—Marketing. I. Title.
HD9773.A2M33   1998
684'.08'068—dc21
                                     98-26021
                                        CIP

Edited by R. Adam Blake and Bruce Stoker
Production edited by Michelle Howry
Cover designed by David Mill, Design Mill
Cover photography by Greg Grosse
Author photo and architectural photography by Ron Iudice

METRIC CONVERSION CHART		
TO CONVERT	**TO**	**MULTIPLY BY**
Inches	Centimeters	2.54
Centimeters	Inches	0.4
Feet	Centimeters	30.5
Centimeters	Feet	0.03
Yards	Meters	0.9
Meters	Yards	1.1
Sq. Inches	Sq. Centimeters	6.45
Sq. Centimeters	Sq. Inches	0.16
Sq. Feet	Sq. Meters	0.09
Sq. Meters	Sq. Feet	10.8
Sq. Yards	Sq. Meters	0.8
Sq. Meters	Sq. Yards	1.2
Pounds	Kilograms	0.45
Kilograms	Pounds	2.2
Ounces	Grams	28.4
Grams	Ounces	0.04

Dedicated to the memory of my father, Carmelo Maccarone

About the Author

Designer, craftsman, author and lecturer Salvatore Maccarone is in a unique woodworking category. A journeyman cabinetmaker with college degrees in both Art and Sculpture from San Jose State University in California, Sal has owned and operated his woodworking company since 1972. For more than a quarter of a century he has been designing and producing "utilitarian art" for both commercial and private clientele in four countries. His work can be seen in many hotels, lobbies and other public areas in the United States, Canada, Cuba and England.

As the author of the book *Tune Up Your Tools* and many magazine and trade journal articles, Sal has documented his personal woodworking techniques for use by schools, maintenance departments and professional woodworkers. His instructional tools are used by others in the industry when teaching woodworking techniques and proper tool maintenance to shop students. Many of Sal's articles and "how-to" furniture plans have been available on the Internet since 1993 for access worldwide by students, teachers and curious clientele.

As a teacher and national seminar speaker, Sal has taught and assisted both hobbyists and professional fellow woodworkers in all parts of the country. On the average of once each month, he visits and speaks to classes on a variety of woodworking topics in one of the twenty-nine major cities he tours. Some of his woodworking topics include, "Woodwork on the Internet," "Tune Up Your Tools," "Limited Edition Furniture," and "Making Money at Woodworking."

Acknowledgments

It is very difficult to acknowledge all the people and forces that influence one's career and contribute to the knowledge necessary to write a book.

In my lifetime I have always had a supportive family who I feel have given me the proper foundation to persevere in whatever I attempt. Because my family is so small, I would like to mention them by name so as to give credit where credit is due. My wife (of twenty eight years), Sharon, and two sons, Sam and Andy, have always given me purpose and the will to do good. My brother Vincent and his family are very dear to me. Lyn Maccarone has always been one of the most positive and supportive people I know, and she is always ready to help me whenever I need. My Aunt Francis, Uncle Dan and cousins Annamarie and Dan make me very proud, and have always supported and been there for me "rain or shine." Bob, Terri, Sonny and Jamie Saltalamachia have also supported me through every phase of my career.

*Carved mahogany doors
by Sal Maccarone, 1991*

C O N T E N T S

CHAPTER

8 Attitude and Working with People   95

Introduction

Almost every good woodworker dreams of becoming a professional and someday being in business for himself. However, the prospect of beginning any business can be overwhelming when one considers all the particulars that are involved. The initial structuring and ongoing concerns which must be attended to should make a person think twice about taking the "quantum leap" and becoming an entrepreneur. On the other hand, given a fundamental foundation, any reasonable-thinking person should not let inexperience with business hold them back, especially if they have something to offer as a woodworker. I have met many qualified craftspersons who are able to produce cost-effective quality products but are reluctant to do their woodwork for a living. For the most part, these people need only a good business overview from someone who has had success.

When I started my woodworking business in 1972, I was young, inexperienced and very naive. I made many mistakes along the way, but somehow I learned by those mistakes and managed to survive and prosper. In retrospect, I realize that had I been able to receive some guidance before beginning my business, I would have saved myself a lot of money and frustration during the early years. As I educated myself both by learning from my mistakes and observing the mistakes of others in business, things began to run a lot more efficiently. There is no reward greater than the satisfaction of running an efficient and successful business of your own. With that in mind, I find it hard to discourage anyone who is willing to learn and has the ambition to "give it a try."

Having always been a teacher, even when I was a student at San Jose State University in California, it's always been important to me that I help others. This is especially true when it comes to helping a fellow woodworker who would like to go into business. I feel that quality woodwork is a "dying" art that needs to be perpetuated by the elders. In these days of plastic composition and mass production, the incentive to do fine work (as a business) is hampered, and slowly being lost. If a lack of basic business knowledge is all that stands in the way of any woodworker who would like to work for himself, it would be a shame for me to look the other way.

One of the questions I am often asked during my woodworking seminars and classes around the country is "Can I make a good living by being in business as a woodworker?" My answer is always "yes." I for one am proud of the fact that I started from scratch with a few basic tools, built a very successful business over the years, raised a family, and at the same time have thoroughly enjoyed the whole experience. Any democratic society affords it citizens the privilege of self-employment; it is up to the individual to succeed. If the individual is dedicated, disciplined and diligent in his or her endeavors there is little reason not to succeed. As in any other situation in life, anyone who is well organized, builds upon a good foundation, and maintains a good attitude will be successful in business.

This book is a result of learning *well* via the business school of "hard knocks." My background in wholesale and retail sales of both production and custom wood products has afforded me a wonderful overview of the entire industry. My past opportunities of teaching and coaching other business woodworkers have dictated the need for a book which approaches the business end of woodworking from a realistic viewpoint. This viewpoint is one that includes basic business formatting coupled with some self-designed marketing strategies, self-discipline and a good attitude. As far as I am concerned, all of these areas are equally important to anyone that is in, or is thinking about being in, business. Unlike most business manuals which may seem dry, I have approached the writing of this book from the heart, and have included the "intangibles" of personality and good will.

An efficient woodworking business includes not only the normal routines of obtaining the proper licenses, daily record keeping and marketing, but also demands good work habits, efficient shop procedures and wise materials acquisition. Without these basic components you can't expect to make a profit at woodworking. You could be the best marketing strategist in the world, but if you cannot produce a product cost effectively, all will be lost. Conversely, you could be a miraculously efficient woodworker, but if you cannot market yourself, or your product, there is no reason for you to go into business. There are many pieces of the puzzle which must fit together to make the whole business run efficiently. This book will take a good look at these many areas of concern which must blend in a way that will result in a successful and ongoing business.

Buona Fortuna E Migiori Auguri,
Salvatore Maccarone

Defining and Planning Your Business

In terms of the tools and techniques that are used, woodworking is simply that—woodworking. But there are many different categories of wordworking as a business, and this fact should play a tremendous part in both the initial planning and the decision-making aspects of any prospective woodworking business. For instance, a custom woodworking shop would not necessarily have the same type of location or square footage concerns as a production woodworking shop. On the other hand, a production shop, as a rule, does not require the same visibility as a custom shop might. Defining the specific operational category of your business as early as possible will do much to help make that business a success.

No person or group of persons should ever enter into any business without a good understanding of what the business is. With woodworking, those criteria are clear-cut and simple. First, some technical ability and/or knowledge should exist. Regardless of whether or not the owner of the business is to be the operator, he or she should at least possess some understanding of how the business is to be operated. Secondly, the business must be defined so that the proper location, shop layout and system of management can be designed to meet that definition. And last, a good market test for a business should be conducted well in advance of its establishment.

No person or group of persons should ever enter into any business without a good understanding of what the business is.

A good market test for a business should be conducted well in advance of its establishment.

TECHNICAL ABILITY AND BUSINESS KNOWLEDGE

Most businesses are born either of demand or entrepreneurial desire. Woodworking is definitely a technical skill type of business. The dictionary defines "technical" as *having to do with the practical, industrial or mechanical arts; or applied sciences*. A technical skill type of business requires persons who are versed in the technicalities of that business. With woodworking, the mechanical knowledge and ability of the woodworkers doing the fabricating are the business's very essence. The operator should also possess a good understanding of the equipment and materials that are being used. If the person who is to be doing the fabricating does not have the proper experience or background, the business will probably not prosper. This may sound cruel, but it is the truth. I have witnessed quite a few individuals enter into

3

business before they have gained the proper knowledge or skills and quickly fail. It can be very difficult to recoup from the financial losses of a business failure. I always recommend that any woodworker gain the proper business experience by working for or observing someone else's business for a period of time *before* entering into business for himself. That period of time will vary according to the individual, but about two years is the minimum. I've had apprentices gain enough knowledge in my shop (coupled with a lot of study on their own time) to begin a successful business of their own in just two years. Other apprentices were still not ready after four years. There is no "rule of thumb" here, but I think that if you are honest with yourself after reading this book, you'll know if you are ready to begin your own woodworking business.

Using Business Skill and Knowledge
In addition to the technical skills required to begin a woodworking business, specific business skills and knowledge are also very important. That's what this book is for. These skills can be developed in advance of starting a business. Formal education is certainly one way to gain an understanding of business, but close observation and actual experience are others. I was an art major in college who had just a few business courses as electives along the way. At that time, I did not place much importance on those courses, but in retrospect I realize that I did gain a good overview of how business works. The ma-

jority of my knowledge, however, was gained by watching how other woodworkers conducted their affairs. This kind of knowledge was more practical for me because it was specific to the woodworking industry. Learning from others' mistakes is always much easier than learning from your own mistakes. When it's appropriate, ask questions of those you work for or acquaintances already in a business that is similar to the one you would like to start. This not only increases your knowledge, but it shows that you care. Most successful people do not mind discussing "how-they-got-started" mistakes they made, their good judgment calls, etc.

WOODSHOP BUSINESS CATEGORIES
Long before signing on the dotted line, you should decide what category of woodworking your business will fall under. Defining a woodworking business in advance is extremely important to success. You don't want to invest in a business unless you are somewhat confident that the physical location is correct, and that the need for your product is there. Are there existing businesses like yours already in the area? If so, is the market for your product saturated, or open to competition? After deciding the business category, these questions should be addressed in a "Product Market Survey" which will be discussed later in this chapter on page 9.

For woodwork fabrication, there are three major categories. The *production shop* produces multiples of the same product; the *custom shop* produces products made to order or on speculation; and the *combination custom/production shop* can cover all of the bases in a given area of woodworking focus. While there are many subcategories to each of these headings, all woodworking shops will fall under one of these three designations (see page 5, "Types of Professional Woodshops"). Certain particulars will be almost

TYPES OF PROFESSIONAL WOODSHOPS
Production Shop

This type of shop is in the business of building multiple copies of the same product. Some examples of work made in this type of shop include:

- Standard kitchen cabinets
- Craft items
- Production furniture (interior and exterior)
- Production doors
- Architectural moulding

Custom Shop

This type of business builds and/or designs custom woodwork items, usually one-of-a-kind pieces for specific clients. Some examples of work from a custom shop would include:

- Custom furniture
- Custom cabinets
- Custom doors
- Wooden sculptures

Custom/Production Shop

This type of business caters to both custom and production clientele. Some examples of combination shops would include:

- Millwork and cabinet shops
- Cabinetmakers
- Custom/standard product lines
- Period furniture shops

the same for all three business types, but each will have specific requirements that should be considered.

Most successful woodworking businesses will evolve at some point after operation has begun. This is only normal! Adjustments will have to be made according to product demand, new product ideas, increases in business, changes in buying trends, etc. Often these adjustments will lead to natural growth, which should translate into more profit. Building a business upon a good foundation, which begins in the planning stages, will help guarantee that natural growth will translate into profit. No one would want to be like the guy who leased 10,000 sq. ft. before the marketability of his product was determined. Or the reverse, say the talented craftsman who only rented 500 sq. ft., without any room for expansion, and then had to move two months later.

> *Building a business upon a good foundation, which begins in the planning stages, will help guarantee that natural growth will translate into profit.*

The Production Shop

Production shops are what the name implies: They're in the business of producing a specific product over and over again. Different products will be introduced from time to time by the addition of new clientele, new product lines, or simply by updating existing products. These types of businesses are normally not concerned with the installation of the products they make. The strictly production shop will only produce the product, and then ship this product to the customers for ultimate distribution or installation.

This type of a business should be in close proximity to the raw material suppliers which are normally located in the industrial areas of town. An industrial location will normally cost less per square foot than a shop right in the heart of town, and will also be closer to shipping and transportation concerns. Industrial locations are often situated outside the city limits. This can mean fewer property taxes and fewer local government controls.

When compared to a custom woodworking

shop with the same yearly gross, the production shop usually requires more physical space. However, it is governed by a much simpler "per part" operating formula (see "Production Shop Operating Formula" below). The less costly physical location requirements will help to offset the need for more space. The production business will spend less time designing, laying out new projects, dealing with clients, and figuring time and material involvement than a custom shop will. Custom shops also have some advantages which will be mentioned later in this chapter.

By their very nature, production businesses usually require some specific equipment. Normally all of the equipment used for production will be industrial quality, or as heavy-duty as possible to withstand hours of use. The basic equipment and tool list will remain the same for any wood shop category, but it is sometimes necessary for production shops to add some "specific use" machinery, such as glue presses, conveyors, boring machinery, tracing lathes, etc. All the equipment particulars should be examined while considering and designing the production space layout.

In addition to the equipment layout, the "flow" of a production shop is extremly impor-

PRODUCTION SHOP

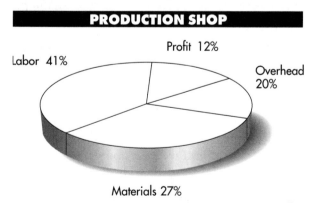

A pie graph shows the basic operating formula for a production woodworking business. The production shop will differ from a custom shop because a bigger percentage of income is typically spent on materials and less on labor. The percentage of profit will also be lower and the overhead higher than in the custom shop.

tant. There should be a definite receiving end and a definite shipping end in any production business. For woodworking, the shop layout in between the material receiving and the product shipping ends should be conducive to a good production flow.

Production flow is defined as *the flow of raw material through the shop as it is being converted into finished product*. Each part of the system should not converge or interfere with any other parts of the operation. In other words, raw materials come in one end and finished products go out the other end with as high a degree of efficiency as possible in the middle.

Efficiency is defined as *the ability to produce the desired effect with a minimum of effort, expense or waste*. Efficiency relates to all aspects of the production woodworking business. It applies to the logistics of receiving materials and shipping finished products, and all things in between. There must be good systems in place for: accounting, which includes both accounts payable and receivable; the ordering of materials; the receiving of materials; the storing of materials; the actual production, which includes employee man-hours, the proper equipment and shop layout; and product distribution. If any of these areas are lacking in efficiency, profits will definitely suffer.

One very important distinction of this production woodworking category is that unless the products being made are absolutely unique, these shops will experience more competition than the custom shops do. For instance, if a city boasts ten shops that produce standard kitchen cabinets of the same type, there will most likely be extreme competition within that category. Survival of the fittest will truly be the case in this type of situation. If a business is efficient, the competition factor can always be offset by a good part yield, or number of finished products that are produced. This is the key to any business, but is extremely important where the production shop is concerned.

The Custom Shop

Custom woodworking shops are in the business of building and/or designing custom woodwork for specific clients. The work is ever changing, depending on the product or material that is "in vogue" at the time, and the type of item that will actually be produced. There are various degrees to which the products themselves will change, but by the nature of the word "custom," in the long run this type of business is destined to change. That is by no means a bad thing. As a matter of fact, in my business the ongoing change is the very reason the work is interesting.

Very often custom shop operators are also licensed contractors. This gives the operators the ability to do the installation of their products. In most states a contractor's license is required for installation. It is a good idea to check with the state agencies about this matter prior to doing any installation. There are a number of liability concerns associated with product installation, so make sure that you are protected under the law before getting involved with this aspect of a custom woodworking business. Clients often prefer to have custom products installed by the shop that measured and built them.

There is more than one school of thought regarding the ideal location for a custom woodworking shop. This type of business definitely needs to be easily accessible to clientele, but doesn't necessarily need a great deal of exposure. The location also needs to be conducive to creativity, or at least reasonably comfortable for the operator.

For instance, for thirteen years I was very fortunate to be able to operate my shop in the middle of a 100-acre woods very close to the center of town. In that case it worked out well for all concerned. My shop was easily accessible to my clients, and at the same time I enjoyed the serenity of a natural setting. This was an extremely rare and ideal situation that not all can enjoy, but do consider yourself in the equation when shopping for a location. Some will say exposure, exposure, exposure, and others will say seclusion, seclusion, seclusion. The point is, there are no set rules regarding the ideal location for a custom woodworking business. If the clientele is established, then it may not be necessary to locate on the main boulevard. If there is some sort of showroom associated with the business, however, then exposure will more than likely be necessary.

The operating formula is not as clear-cut for the custom shop as with the production shop. There is much more personal involvement with the clientele which certainly equates to more total time spent on the projects (see "Custom Shop Operating

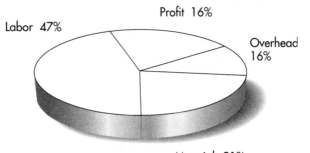

A pie graph shows the basic operating formula for a custom woodworking business. This formula differs from that of a production shop because more labor in the form of "time" is typically spent with clientele. A smaller percentage of the gross income will be spent on materials, and there is a bigger profit margin than with a production shop.

Formula," p. 7). Laying out the individual projects, taking field measurements, and locating and securing a variety of materials for each separate project also contribute to the formula. All these variables make it much more difficult to accurately estimate costs. This process is certainly an art, and must be cultivated. In chapter four, "Estimating, Bidding and Pricing Your Work," I will explore some estimating formulas.

The bottom line difference between custom and production work is that it costs much more to produce custom work, and consequently more must be charged. The trade-off between custom and production work is that custom work provides more product variety, while production work requires less contact with individual clients and deals with clear-cut products. Each woodworker is different when it comes to what he or she is comfortable producing. I know of many wonderful woodworkers who could not do what I do when it comes to dealing with people. I, on the other hand, am not happy producing the same product over and over. We all like to work with wood and should feel privileged earning a living at what we like to do, but we should try to build on what comes naturally within our field.

The Combination Custom and Production Shop

A combination custom and production shop operates similarly to the other two categories. Com-

bination shops are in the business of catering to both markets. There are many renditions of this kind of business. One example would be the custom cabinet shop that produces a line of standard cabinets that can also be ordered in specific configurations, sizes or materials. This type of business is seldom owned and operated by a single individual. Usually requiring separate entities for sales, marketing, shop operations, shipping and accounting, this business is one of the toughest to control. Because of the "dual focus" of this type of business, there is sometimes just too much ground for one person to cover.

Very few woodworking businesses start as a combination shop. They normally begin as either a production shop or a custom shop. In order to succeed, the combination shop should either be allowed to grow naturally or be structured by very experienced key persons. In other words, this type of "full-blown" business should not even be considered as a first-time endeavor. With all the requirements of both business types wrapped up in one, it can be very expensive and hard to organize the combination shop from scratch.

The operating formula (see "Custom/Production Shop Operating Formula" below) for a combination business is similar to that of a purely custom or purely production shop in most regards.

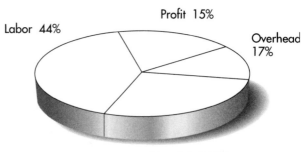

CUSTOM/PRODUCTION SHOP

Profit 15%
Labor 44%
Overhead 17%
Materials 24%

A pie graph shows the basic operating formula for a custom/production woodworking business. This shop averages in all areas between the strictly custom and strictly production shop.

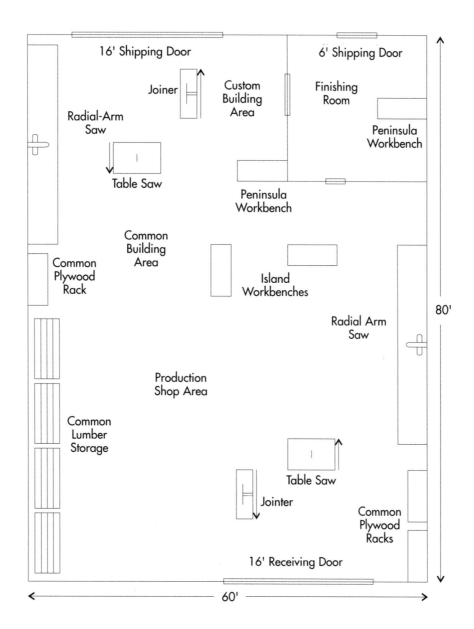

16' Shipping Door

Joiner

Custom
Building
Area

6' Shipping Door

Finishing
Room

Radial-Arm
Saw

Peninsula
Workbench

Table Saw

Peninsula
Workbench

Common
Building
Area

Common
Plywood
Rack

Island
Workbenches

Radial Arm
Saw

80'

Production
Shop Area

Common
Lumber
Storage

Table Saw

Jointer

Common
Plywood
Racks

16' Receiving Door

60'

An efficient layout for a combination woodworking shop would include common areas for material storage, receiving, product finishing and shipping.

Because this is an "overlap" type of business, the operating formula is complicated by having two businesses in one. For instance, there are likely to be two distinct categories of employees involved— the specialized mechanics, and the specific machinery operators. The accounting for this type of business is also more difficult. There should be two individual sets of books: one for the custom aspect and one for the production aspect.

If on-site installation is part of the combination business, which it normally is, a contractor's license may be required. As mentioned above, check with your state agencies that govern contractors for information regarding product installation. Some combination shops "sub out" the installation aspect of their business to a subcontractor so as not to get involved with installation. It's all a matter of how the particular business is structured and who the clients are.

Unless the combination shop focuses on just

Making Your Basic Business Plan

A basic business plan should be made prior to organizing or beginning actual business operations. Follow these steps to develop your own plan:

1. Develop a realistic *vision* for the business in terms of size, activities and appearance.
2. Write a *mission* statement which indicates the purposes of the business.
3. Determine the long-term and short-term *objectives* of the business.
4. Plan the operational and marketing *strategies* by which the vision, mission and objectives will be achieved.
5. Set time-based *goals* for implementing the strategies.
6. Determine the *venues* which will be used to implement the strategies.
7. List the *values* and *ethics* to which your business will adhere to attract and retain customers.

one job at a time, which would be very rare, a lot of space will be required. Every situation is unique, but for some of these shops it is necessary to operate two distinct departments, one for production and one for custom work. In this case each department would have its own basic tools, layout areas, and building stations in order to be efficient. Common areas for material storage and "intermittent use" machinery, such as surface planers, endless belt sanders, etc., can be conveniently located to both departments. All of this requires space! For this reason, and all the other reasons cited above for the *production shop*, location in the industrial area of town is recommended.

MAKING A BUSINESS PLAN

Before entering into a new business, the owner or owners should always make a business plan.

A business plan is a written summary of the business proposed. It should provide all the information necessary to evaluate the business. The amount of information will depend on the complexity of the business. The table below lists the many key areas that any business plan should include.

The space required for the proposed operation, the tools required, and the supplies and materials that will be necessary to begin operation are just some of the areas relevant to all woodworking businesses. When doing a business plan, all things should be considered and the plan should be completed well in advance of beginning the business. Standard business plan formats can be customized to suit just about any type of woodworking business. These basic standard forms can usually be obtained from a library, the Internet or any major bank.

PRODUCT MARKET SURVEY

A product market survey is a test of the market (local or otherwise) for a particular product. This is not to be confused with product marketing, which takes place after the business has begun. A good businessperson will make it a point to know, within reason, what the demand for a particular proposed product will be. You should never go into business simply because you personally like the product which is being considered. Some sort of product market test should be performed in advance of operations. Market testing can be done in several simple ways. Depending on the scope and capacity of the prospective business, anything from simply talking to prospective clientele to studying past, present and future demographics can constitute a market test.

There are many areas to explore when conducting a product market test. First and foremost, does the basic need for the particular product or category of product exist? For instance, you

Personality/Ability Test

This simple test will help indicate which woodworking business category suits you best. See page 12 for the results.

1. What is your main reason for wanting to go into business?
   - ❑ a.) You want to make money.
   - ❑ b.) You want to be independent.
   - ❑ c.) You are tired of your present line of work.
   - ❑ d.) You hate your present boss.

2. As far as you are concerned:
   - ❑ a.) A woodworking business should be easy.
   - ❑ b.) A woodworking business would be difficult.
   - ❑ c.) You'll do whatever it takes to have your own woodworking business.
   - ❑ d.) You are not sure if it would be easy or hard.

3. You consider your woodworking abilities to be:
   - ❑ a.) lousy but you are willing to learn;
   - ❑ b.) better than average;
   - ❑ c.) moderate but you are willing to improve;
   - ❑ d.) as good as the next person's.

4. Your idea of financing a woodworking business is:
   - ❑ a.) borrow the money and buy all that you need;
   - ❑ b.) save the necessary money before you begin;
   - ❑ c.) begin with some borrowed money and some that you have saved;
   - ❑ d.) start with nothing; the money should roll in.

5. Your idea of a good location for your business is:
   - ❑ a.) in an industrial area of town;
   - ❑ b.) in the woods somewhere;
   - ❑ c.) on the main street of town;
   - ❑ d.) in your garage.

6. You relate to people:
   - ❑ a.) well, but you don't like to be bothered while you are working;
   - ❑ b.) in an average way;
   - ❑ c.) wonderfully, anytime;
   - ❑ d.) not so well.

7. You consider the designing aspect of woodworking to be:
   - ❑ a.) not really an important part of woodworking;
   - ❑ b.) as important a part of woodworking as technical ability;
   - ❑ c.) more important than technical ability;
   - ❑ d.) less important than technical ability.

8. What approach would you take to selling your work?
   - ❑ a.) Go door to door and talk to everyone.
   - ❑ b.) Have a showroom attached to your shop.
   - ❑ c.) Do a good job and wait for referrals.
   - ❑ d.) Spend a lot of money on advertising.

9. In starting a woodworking business, you feel as if:
   - ❑ a.) you should go in with someone who has more expertise than yourself;
   - ❑ b.) you would like to open and run a business by yourself;
   - ❑ c.) you should form a group of several people with varied skills;
   - ❑ d.) you would like to own a business alone, but do only part of the work.

10. Your attitude about tools is:
   - ❑ a.) You would like to have the top of the line for every aspect of the business.
   - ❑ b.) It doesn't really matter because the tools are only as good as the operator.
   - ❑ c.) You will buy what you can afford at the time and/or when you need it.
   - ❑ d.) Tools don't really matter that much.

11. As far as clientele are concerned:
   - ❑ a.) You don't really care who you work for.
   - ❑ b.) You would like to cater to the rich.
   - ❑ c.) You would like to cater to the middle class.
   - ❑ d.) You would like to cater to the poor.

12. As far as the work itself is concerned:
   - ❑ a.) You enjoy producing many copies of the same product.
   - ❑ b.) You don't like to make the same things over and over.
   - ❑ c.) You don't really care what you are making as long as you are making something for a profit.
   - ❑ d.) All woodworking is easy for you.

Product Market Testing Strategies

A market test will indicate the need for a product. So, prior to introducing a new product, you should test the market by doing one or more of the following:

- Interview your clients
- Interview your competitors
- Run low-cost advertisements
- Evaluate the demographics of your targeted marketing area
- Display prototypes of the product to elicit customer opinions

wouldn't want to go into the production cabinet business in a town with a dwindling population of one thousand unless you heard that IBM was moving in next year. On the other hand, if your market study indicates steady growth for the next ten years, cabinets just might be a great business to consider.

The Results of the Test are as Follows:

The scores should be tallied in terms of how many *a*'s, *b*'s, *c*'s, and *d*'s you marked. If you marked mostly *a*'s, you would be best suited for a production shop. If you marked mostly *b*'s, you would be best suited to a custom shop. If you marked mostly *c*'s, you could consider a custom/production shop. If you marked mostly *d*'s, you should keep your day job.

> *A good businessperson will make it a point to know, within reason, what the demand for a particular proposed product will be by conducting some sort of market test.*

CHAPTER SUMMARY

- All successful businesses are built on a good foundation. A good foundation includes: knowing the business category, which will help determine the right physical location; understanding the operation; preparing a good business plan; and conducting a market test in advance of beginning the business.

- In order for a business to be successful, good fundamental planning is very important. Technical ability and business knowledge are the mainstay of any successful woodworking business. Ability and knowledge can be gained in several ways, such as studying, asking questions and hands-on experience. Working for someone else for a period of time will help one gain business experience and technical ability.

- There are three major categories in the woodworking business: the production shop, the custom shop, and the combination custom/production shop. It is important to determine which category your proposed or existing business falls into. There is always room to evolve and expand, but a solid beginning in one of these categories is important to success.

- Making a business plan is important for more than one reason. An honest business plan helps one to understand every aspect of a proposed business. A business plan is also required for any initial or future financing of the business. Making a business plan in advance saves time and money in the future.

- Product market testing is a means of intelligently determining if there is a need for the product. This can be done in several simple ways or can be as detailed as needed. In any event, the results of the market test can be included in the business plan which will be impressive to all concerned.

2

Legal Entities and Organizing a Business

Organizing a business in terms of its specific legal definition, or legal entity, is a most important first step in actually setting up any business concern. Once all the conceptual planning is done it will be time to "roll up your sleeves" and make some decisions which include assigning a legal definition to the business. Working on your own or with partners, silent or otherwise, is a big part of this equation. Among other things, the forming of any business entity will involve five factors.

- The need for capital
- Any legal restrictions or mandates
- The number of owners
- Tax advantages
- Assumed liabilities

The legal definition that is decided on can have a great impact on how you are protected under the law. This decision will also determine income tax rules and regulations. For the purposes of this book, and specifically a woodworking business, I would like to explore three basic forms of business organizations: *sole proprietorships*, *partnerships* and *corporations*. There are literally vol-

> *Organizing a business in terms of its specific legal definition, or legal entity, is a most important first step in actually setting up any business concern.*

> *Anytime there is more than one person involved in a business, it is important to have a written agreement.*

umes written elsewhere about this subject, which only goes to show that there is much to consider.

After reading the cursory information that follows, it may pay to do some additional research and/or to consult a business attorney before making your final decision.

If you intend to set up a business as the sole owner, it will certainly be easier than if more than one owner is involved. Anytime there is more than one person involved in a business, it is important to have a written agreement. This document would detail in part how business decisions are to be made and how any profits or losses would be handled. This agreement would also detail what would happen upon the death, insolvency or termination of a partner or shareholder, and what procedure would be followed if someone wanted to sell his interest. These kinds of things should be decided upon "up front," considering that later everyone may not still be on friendly terms.

If you elect to research this subject on your own, there are many additional sources of free information. Here are a few of the easiest sources to access:

- The local public library
- College and university libraries
- The Internet (which can also be accessed at most public libraries)
- The Small Business Administration (SBA)
- Business publications (periodicals)
- Woodworking trade associations

SOLE PROPRIETORSHIPS

Currently, there are reported to be some 22 million small businesses in the United States, and approximately 15.5 million of those are run as sole proprietorships. A sole proprietorship is typically owned and operated by one individual or a married couple. The individual or individuals are the sole owner; hence the name sole proprietorship. This type of business is really not considered to be a legal entity, in itself, under the law. Technically, a sole proprietorship is an extension of the individual who owns and operates the business. Obviously, this makes the owner directly responsible for the debts and any other liabilities incurred by the business. On the other hand, the owner has total possession of all the business assets. The business income or business loss of a sole proprietorship will then be combined with all other earnings of that individual for income tax purposes.

A sole proprietorship is the least costly and simplest way of beginning a business. Technically, someone could form a business such as this by simply finding a location, obtaining the proper licenses and hanging out a sign. In the case of a sole proprietorship, one is truly "working for himself," and there can be a lot of personal satisfaction associated with the business. This form of business also offers the most decision-making control of the three business types, but there is absolutely no legal or financial protection between you and your business. There are really no tax benefits either, except for being able to claim business losses on your personal income tax for a period of time.

If a business attorney is used for the initial setup of a sole proprietorship, the fees will be less than for the other two types of business entities because there will be a minimum of documents to prepare. The accounting procedures are also less stringent than in partnerships or corporations. There are some minimal costs for registering the business name and obtaining a state and/or local business license (where applicable). Most

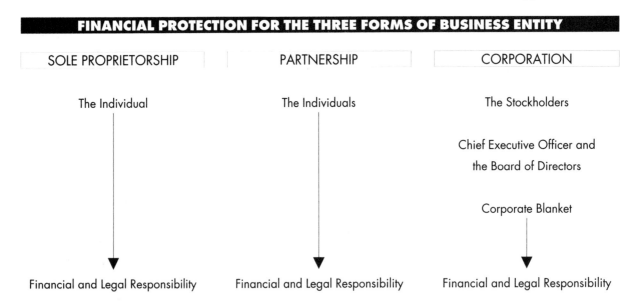

FINANCIAL PROTECTION FOR THE THREE FORMS OF BUSINESS ENTITY

SOLE PROPRIETORSHIP	PARTNERSHIP	CORPORATION
The Individual	The Individuals	The Stockholders
		Chief Executive Officer and the Board of Directors
		Corporate Blanket
Financial and Legal Responsibility	Financial and Legal Responsibility	Financial and Legal Responsibility

ADVANTAGES AND DISADVANTAGES OF A SOLE PROPRIETORSHIP

Advantages

- It is the easiest to get started because there are minimal legal and registration requirements to begin and maintain this type of business.
- There is the greatest freedom of action and maximum authority because the sole proprietor has total decision-making capability.
- The sole proprietor enjoys all the benefits and/or profit of the business.
- All the assets of the business are owned by the sole proprietor unless they are purchased by a loan or lease.
- Losses from the business can be applied to the personal income of the sole proprietor which may be an advantage (for a while) if there are other sources of income.

Disadvantages

- There is unlimited liability because the sole proprietor is personally responsible for all the business liabilities. These liabilities include all contracts, debts, losses, expenses or any other financial responsibilities of the business and all actions of the business's employees.
- The sole proprietor is personally responsible for any lawsuits against the business.
- Income from the business must be included with other sources of income of the sole proprietor for the year.
- Growth is always limited to personal energies and illness can endanger the business.

states and some local jurisdictions require a license in order to open a business regardless of the business entity, and for certain types of woodworking, especially where installation of products is involved, some states require a specific contractor's license.

There are some definite advantages and disadvantages of a sole proprietorship, (see "Advantages and Disadvantages of a Sole Proprietorship" above). A sole proprietorship exists when an individual carries on business for the individual's own benefit. A sole proprietor does not include

> *A "golden rule" of any partnership is that each of the partners has a duty to act in good faith toward the other partners. This is also called a "fiduciary duty."*

other people in the business except as employees. In terms of the continuity of a sole proprietorship, if the owner is disabled, the business will suffer unless family members, friends or employees can cover for the owner. The death of a sole proprietor will terminate the business as it exists. Heirs can of course inherit and liquidate the assets or start a new business using the same assets and/or location.

PARTNERSHIPS

A partnership exists as a business when two or more individuals or business entities (sole proprietor or corporation) come together with common goals as a business for profit. The members of this business entity are called the partners, and hence the name partnership. This type of business entity is quite similar to a sole proprietorship, but has two or more proprietors. The partners together would be referred to as a firm, company or partnership, and the business name would be the firm, partnership or company name. Many small businesses will use this form of entity for various reasons, and there are distinct advantages and disadvantages to forming a partnership, (see "Advantages and Disadvantages of a Partnership" below).

A "golden rule" of any partnership is that each of the partners has a duty to act in good faith toward the other partners. This is also called a "fiduciary duty." A partner should not take advantage of any opportunities or information obtained while involved in the partnership for personal use without the permission of the other partners. Also, a partner should not carry on a separate competitive business at the same time that a partnership exists without prior consent from the other partners. All partners are also accountable to each other when it comes to the business of that partnership.

A partnership can be formed simply by the making of an oral agreement between two or more persons, but this is not recommended. It is a good idea to have a business attorney or some other knowledgeable person draw up a formal partnership agreement so that future disputes, should they arise, can be settled without problems. The rights, responsibilities, obligations and term (length of time) of the partnership should be detailed within a partnership agreement. Property that is purchased by the partnership is called "partnership property," and is owned by the partnership according to the partnership agreement. Keep in mind that usually while conceiving a partnership the principle players are friends, or at least friendly toward one another. It is still a good idea, however, to get all of the "rules" pertaining to the future business down on paper so that there are no major problems after the business is formed and operating. This simple first step will help keep everyone on friendly terms and maintain mutual respect throughout the duration of the partnership.

A partnership is a legal entity recognized under the law with rights and responsibilities in and of itself. For instance, a partnership can obtain credit, sign contracts, sue or be sued. Partnerships must file a "fictitious" business name which is the name the business will "do business as." The filing procedures for the fictitious name are different in every state, but basically they require that after registration an advertisement be placed in an accredited newspaper for some period of time, (usually three to four weeks). This ad will include

ADVANTAGES AND DISADVANTAGES OF A PARTNERSHIP

Advantages:

- It is much easier to organize than a corporation.
- It has separate legal status.
- There is shared responsibility (two or more heads are usually better than one).
- There are additional sources of venture capital.
- It has a better credit rating than a corporation of similar size.
- Profits are taxed only once at partner's rate.

Disadvantages:

- There is unlimited liability to general partners.
- Decision making is divided. Control is shared among the partners, which is a situation that could lead to disputes.
- You are responsibile for the partners' actions as well as your own.
- There is possible death, withdrawal or bankruptcy of a partner.
- It is difficult to "get rid" of a bad partner.
- There is a hazy line of authority.

the names and addresses of everyone involved in the partnership, and will serve as public notice that these individuals will be doing business under this company name. The ad also allows time for any other business entity with the same name to object to you. A partnership is also required to file a federal income tax return, Form 1065, although the partnership itself does not typically pay the income tax. Information from the partnership return is combined with the personal income of the separate partners on their individual personal tax returns.

General and Limited Partnerships

There are two different forms of partnerships, general and limited. A general partnership exists when two or more individuals run a business enterprise together. Each of the partners has some ownership of the company assets, and each is responsible for the partnership liabilities. The general partners all have authority in running the business according to their partnership agreement. The liability can also be defined under the agreement, but when push comes to shove, banks and creditors usually have recourse to the personal assets of all partners.

A limited partnership exists when one or more general partners, and one or more limited partners, come together to do business. In the case of a limited partnership, a general partner is personally liable for partnership debts, and a limited partner contributes capital and shares in the profit or losses. The limited partners do not take part in running the business and are not personally liable for any debts incurred by the partnership. Limited partners are sometimes called "silent partners."

A partnership can be terminated in several different ways:

- If there is a predetermined term or function assigned to the existence of the partnership, it will be terminated on that date or upon completion of the function.
- Upon written notice of any partner.
- Upon the death or insolvency of any of the partners.
- If ordered to terminate by any court for any reason.

CORPORATIONS

A corporation is a legal entity which is separated by law from its owners and stockholders. For this reason, many people prefer to carry on business as a corporation. The owners and shareholders are protected by law from the liabilities of the corporation, but creditors often require personal guarantees of the principal owners (of small corporations) before they will extend any credit to that corporation. Any small business entity, especially a corporation, must have a reasonable amount of liability insurance or the corporate veil can be broken, and managers, officers and board members can be held personally responsible for the activities of the corporation.

> *Any small business entity, especially a corporation, must have a reasonable amount of liability insurance or the corporate veil can be broken, and managers, officers and board members can be held personally responsible for the activities of the corporation.*

A corporation has almost all the legal rights of an individual and is responsible for its own liabilities and debts. Corporations must file their own separate corporate income tax returns (Form 1120) and are directly responsible for paying the taxes on any income that is derived from operations.

Corporations can be formed and owned by one person or be quite large and have two different types of shareholders. There are "common" shareholders and "preference shareholders." Preference shares give the holders certain rights that common shareholders do not have. For instance, preference shareholders may receive profits from the corporation before the common shareholders, but they may not have a voice in how the corporation is run. The rights and privileges of both kinds of shareholders can be designated in any way the corporate charter dictates. Decision-making control depends on stock ownership. In small corporations, where there are only a few owners, 51 percent of stock ownership allows the owner to make policy decisions, although this control must still be exercised through regular board of directors' meetings, and records must be kept of these decisions.

A corporation is formed by filing Articles of Incorporation with the secretary of state, which usually requires the help of a business attorney. A fictitious name must be filed, and the corporation will do business under that name. Bylaws must be written and adopted, a board of directors must be elected, and shares of stock issued. The board of directors basically runs the company on a day-to-day basis. Regular director and shareholder meetings must be held, and minutes must be taken at those meetings. The decisions that are made at the meetings must be put into the form of written resolutions.

The incorporation of a business has its own set of advantages and disadvantages (see "Advantages and Disadvantages of a Corporation" at right). There is individual protection from creditors but a loss of personal decision-making authority. The initial start-up expenses can be outweighed by the fact that there is legal protection for all the owners as individuals, but the officers

ADVANTAGES AND DISADVANTAGES OF A CORPORATION

Advantages:

- There is limited liability of the owners and shareholders (not always true for small corporations).
- Taxation of the corporation is separate from that of the owners and shareholders and sometimes at a lower taxation rate.
- The corporation can bring in additional capital through the sale of equity, or allow an individual to sell or transfer his interest in the business.
- The corporation can initiate lawsuits (or be sued) in the corporation name.
- The continuity of a corporation can be ongoing even after the death of an owner or shareholder.

Disadvantages:

- There are much higher legal start-up costs. Decision making is divided (power limited by bylaws and a charter) and there is maximum accountability.
- Corporation tax returns must be filed, and minutes must be recorded of all regular meetings.
- Losses that are incurred during the start-up years cannot be claimed by the stockholders on their personal tax returns.

of a corporation can still be held liable to the stockholders for any improper actions.

PART-TIME VS. FULL-TIME BUSINESSES

Regardless of the legal definition or entity of a business, it can be operated as many hours a week as the owner or owners wish. The number of hours worked will define the business as full- or part-time. This factor will also help to dictate where the business should be operated from. Many very important corporations started as part-time businesses in a garage, and then grew "naturally" into full-time concerns according to the success of the business or desire of the owners.

Technically speaking, a part-time business would be any business which operates less than forty hours a week. A full-time business operates forty hours a week or more. Another example of a part-time business would be one in which two or more owners each apply less than forty hours a week. In this case the individual owners are applying part-time effort while maybe working the rest of the work week at a different concern. Many businesses are set up to continue to operate as part time, as in the case of retired individuals who just enjoy woodworking and do not want to work full time anymore.

> *In the woodworking industry many people begin a private business while they are "gainfully" employed elsewhere.*

In the woodworking industry many people begin a private business while they are "gainfully" employed elsewhere. As suggested in chapter one, this is probably a wise way to begin a business. It gives owners a chance to "get on their feet" with a business and, at the same time, find out if there is enough of a market for the proposed products. This approach can keep business overhead at a minimum while owners are acquiring the equipment necessary for a woodworking shop. It will also allow them to hone their skills while working elsewhere.

In any event, if a business exists full or part time, it has to be defined for tax purposes. Taxes include federal and state income taxes as well as state sales tax (in most states) in the case of retail sales. When a business owner is employed full time at his own business, there is also a federal self-employment tax which must be paid. This tax is for Social Security and Medicare, and is based on the profit that the business produces during any given year. The Small Business Adminstration can be contacted for information about income, sales and self-employment taxes.

CHAPTER SUMMARY

- All businesses must be organized and have a legal definition. There are three types of business organizations: the sole proprietorship, the partnership and the corporation. The forming of any of these three business entities will involve five factors: the need for capital, legal restrictions, number of owners, tax advantages and assumed liabilities.

- The sole proprietorship is the easiest to set up and most common of the three types of business organizations. There are minimal legal and registration requirements to begin a business such as this. There is also the greatest freedom of action and maximum authority, but at the same time, an unlimited liability. The sole proprietor owns all the assets of the business and does not have to share the profits, but must absorb the losses. For income tax purposes, the profits from this type of business will be added to the personal income of the sole proprietor, and the losses can be deducted.

- A partnership is used when two or more people go into business together and do not want to form a corporation. A written agreement should be made before the business begins to spell out all the details of the partnership. It is similar to a sole proprietorship in that the profits and losses are dealt with in the individual's tax returns. As a true business entity, it has a separate legal status. A partnership usually has a better credit rating than a corporation of similar size because the partners are personally responsible for the debts. Partners are responsible for each other's actions, and have a fiduciary duty towards one another.

- A corporation is a legal entity which is separated by law from its stockholders. Corporations are responsible for their own debts and liabilities and must file tax returns. A corporation must directly pay the taxes on any profits. The continuity of this form of business can be uninterrupted even after the death of a stockholder. It is more expensive to begin a business like this because of the legal forms which must be filed. Corporation losses cannot be claimed by the stockholders on their personal tax returns.

- A business is considered to be parttime if it is operated, or its owners each operate it, less than forty hours a week. It may be wise to begin a woodworking business parttime while gainfully employed elsewhere. This approach can keep the overhead down, while one acquires the tools and equipment necessary to run a full-time business. All the taxation that applies to a full-time business will still apply to a part-time business.

3

Finances, Vendors, Business Assets and Employees

In my career I have had the good fortune of meeting many capable woodworkers all around the country. Many of them would have no problem operating a shop, but are reluctant to go into business because they lack a good understanding of finances. Lack of this knowledge is an understandable reason for making a person think twice about entering business. While formal business courses are always nice to have under your belt, they are not necessarily mandatory for entering business at the beginning level. What is really needed is some good fundamental knowledge of finances and how they work, a good accountant, and some direction for finding the right answers. This is the intent of this chapter.

Conducting financial operations is the essence of business. An understanding of basic business finances is especially helpful when a business begins to grow. Building assets while regular operations are continuing is how a business grows. How to make the best use of the business assets is every good businessperson's dilemma, but it can be the key to accomplishing goals. Financial transactions associated with business include:

- Credit
- Loans
- Contracts
- Taxes
- Leases
- Bank accounts and payroll

> *Building assets while regular operations are continuing is how a business grows.*

The purpose of this chapter is to give an overview of financing, taxes and employee financial concerns for a woodworking business. The confines of this chapter will not allow for more than a good foundation—to cover these topics in depth, I would have to devote a book to each of them. Therefore, my overview should be used as "food for thought" when pursuing financing and deciding matters concerning taxes and employees. Local banks and lending institutions can provide additional information to help with your decisions on financing. For tax and employee information, it is highly recommended that a good local accountant or the Small Business Administration be contacted prior to the actual structuring of a business. If your business already exists and you are considering future plans or trying to refine your present operation, it is not too late to redesign your present structure.

WORKING WITH BANKS AND LENDING INSTITUTIONS

All banks and lending institutions are in business to make money, and they have competition within their industry as we do. We are their customers, and they should treat us as we would treat our customers and patrons. Because they are in business, formal lenders will structure their loans so that the return on money invested (loans) is equal to or greater than the risk factors that are involved. If the risk of helping to capitalize a new business or the expansion of an existing business is perceived to be great, the interest rate charged will be higher than for a lower-risk situation. With that thought in mind you should understand how lenders perceive risk before you present a business loan proposal.

There are many factors that make up the whole risk equation in the eyes of a lender. First they consider the amount of risk or collateral that the business owner is willing to pledge or commit. The motivation to repay the loan is the "comfort zone" that lenders consider when assigning an interest rate to the situation. The more assets committed by the applicant, the more comfortable (or secure) the lender will be. The types of security that make a lender comfortable depend on the amount of capital requested and the track record of the business or person seeking the loan. Lenders adjust the committed security according to its liquidity, or the ease at which the collateral can be converted to cash in the event of a default. The liquid value of the collateral will also affect the interest rate and approval of the loan. Collateral for business loans in the woodworking industry would include:

Liens on property (real estate)—deeds of trust
Debentures—a bond against business property (equipment, fixtures)
Accounts receivable—money owed the business

Contract liens—a promissory note based upon a project contract that is already in effect

Because lending institutions are in competition, it is wise to shop for the best interest rate possible. In putting together a loan package, ¼ of a percent difference in the interest rate may save a substantial sum of money when considering the duration of the loan. It is also wise to deal with people who are familiar with you (as a person) and your business. Formal lenders are people, and a good personal relationship with them can do wonders where the timing and structuring of a loan are concerned. When applying for a business loan, remember that if one lender turns you down, that doesn't necessarily mean they all will. There are many banks to choose from, some of which are more familiar with a specific industry or may assess your business situation differently.

LOANS AND OTHER TYPES OF CREDIT

When a business is successful, thoughts usually turn toward growth. Before serious growth can take place, however, space and capital will be needed. Sometimes the physical problem of needed space cannot be rectified until the capital for expansion is secured. When capital is needed to expand operations in anticipation of future sales fulfillment or growth of any kind, there are several options which can be explored. Bank loans are the traditional means by which "working" capital is obtained because loans are usually cheaper than lines of credit, which often must be paid off in one lump sum. On the other hand, funds are much easier to access with established lines of credit because bank loans are much more formal. For the businessperson, the trade-off between cost and convenience must be weighed each time a need for capital arises.

Loans for new businesses are much more difficult to obtain than for established ones. As a rule, banks will require two to three years of operation before they will make a loan using business assets as collateral (security for the loan). Until that time, personal assets (such as home equity or other real estate) will be used to secure any financing for a business. Regardless of the business circumstance, the loan process is always the same. A formal loan application is filled out and must be accompanied by a financial history (profit and loss statements) of an existing business. If the business is new or still conceptual, personal tax returns and a list of personal liabilities will be needed along with a plan for how the money will be used (see "Making a Business Plan" in chapter one). The last ingredient of the loan application package is a specific plan for how the money will be paid back. An existing business with a track record can often use a simple cash flow projection to meet the payback plan requirements. It is wise to use the services of a business accountant in preparing a formal bank loan application.

Types of Loans

Depending on the type of business, there is a particular method of financing which would most benefit the business entity. When borrowing money, it is always best to pay it back in the most timely manner without detriment to the business. Each time a financial business commitment is resolved per "the terms of the agreement," a favorable rating is entered into the business credit history. Conversely, if the terms are not met by the business, a less than favorable mark is entered into the credit report. For these reasons it is im-

When borrowing money, it is always best to pay it back in the most timely manner without detriment to the business.

portant to design the terms of the agreement to be as realistic for the business to handle as possible. There are several categories of business loans available which include:

Short-term loans—a common type of business loan designed to be paid off in a year. These loans are considered when interim working capital is needed and are typically repaid in one lump sum when accounts receivable or inventory are converted into cash.

Intermediate-term loans—often used for start-up, expansion or working capital. They are designed to be paid off in one to three years, are usually "reduced" monthly or quarterly, and are paid off in full at the end of the term.

Long-term loans—usually used for start-ups, major improvements, acquiring assets, and new equipment. The term of these loans is usually from three to five years and payments are made monthly or quarterly.

Lines of credit—used at will for a variety of capital needs. These are a valuable asset to a business. These loans must be cleared at least once a year and do not require an application each time money is borrowed. Lenders will re-evaluate financial statements periodically and adjust the credit line accordingly.

Small Business Administration loans—designed for small businesses that do not qualify for a typical bank loan. Participating banks are guaranteed up to 80 percent of the loan to a qualifying small business owner. These loans are usually long-term loans which are paid monthly.

THE SMALL BUSINESS ADMINISTRATION

The Small Business Administration (SBA) was started in the United States in 1953. The primary goal of this organization is to help small business owners start and build a strong business. The fact that there are twenty-two million small businesses in America which employ 50 percent of the private work force is good reason for the existence of this important entity. Small businesses generate more than half of the nation's gross domestic product and are the principle source of new jobs. This agency can help the small business owner in a variety of ways. The SBA has an answer desk, which is a toll free information center, that can answer questions about starting or running a small business and how to get assistance. The answer desk, (800-8-ASK-SBA) is an automated system which can be accessed twenty-four hours a day, seven days a week, but there are desk operators (real people) available Monday through Friday from 9 A.M. to 5 P.M. eastern standard time. The SBA also has a Web site at (http://www.sba.gov). In addition, there are SBA district offices in every state (see the list of regional, district and branch offices of the SBA in the Appendix), which can be contacted for in-person service and advice. Some of the small business services that the SBA provides include:

Management-Assistance Aids—The SBA produces and maintains a library of publications and videos which are available at a nominal cost.

Business Counseling and Training—The Service Corps of Retired Executives is a group of volunteers who provide expert advice on every aspect of business.

Small Business Development Centers (SBDCs)—Funded by the SBA in cooperation with the academic community, the private sector and state and local governments, these centers can help you to prepare SBA loan applications.

One-Stop Capital Shops (OSCSs)—An SBA contribution to the Empowerment Zones/Enterprise Communities program, OSCSs target resources to selected distressed communities and address an array of social and economic needs. They provide access to a full range of SBA financial and technical assistance programs as well as those of other federal agencies, state and local governments and the private sector.

Lending Programs—The SBA provides financial assistance in the form of loan guarantees rather than direct loans. The SBA will guarantee up to 80 percent of loan repayment; these loans are generally administered by participating banks.

Women's Prequalification Loan—This program enables the SBA to prequalify a loan guaranty for a woman business owner before she approaches a lender. The program focuses on an applicant's character, credit, experience and reliability rather than her collateral.

CAPLines—This program offers five types of loans to finance the short-term, cyclical working capital needs of small businesses. The loan proceeds generally will be advanced against a borrower's existing or anticipated inventory and/or accounts receivable.

FA$TRAK—This pilot program provides additional incentive to lenders to make small business loans. Participating banks use their own documentation and procedures to approve, service and liquidate loans of up to $100,000 in return for SBA guarantees of up to 50 percent of each loan.

NEGOTIATING LOANS AND LEASES

One of the most important things any business owner can develop is negotiation skills. No one

> *One of the most important things any business owner can develop is negotiation skills.*
>
> ———
>
> *When it comes to a financial matter with bankers or landlords, confidence with* exact *figures is very important.*

is born with these skills, but they are very important in business. The decisions that are made during important financial negotiations may have to be lived with for a long time. Project contract proposals, which are discussed in chapter four, are a written form of negotiation. All negotiations are a process of give and take and the final agreement usually favors the best negotiator. This negotiation, or refinement process, is the only window of opportunity that will exist prior to a completed contract or agreement. In any transaction that will affect the future financial matters of a business, it is wise to be, or have access to, the best negotiator possible.

A person who is best prepared with current and correct information will have the edge in any negotiation. When it comes to a financial matter with bankers or landlords, confidence with *exact* figures is very important. Guessing during critical negotiations can not only prove to be embarrassing but may also cost the unprepared negotiator his position. A prepared negotiator will try to anticipate questions and have a preplanned response to those questions. For example, if a long-term lease for a shop space is being negotiated, it would be wise to know what comparable spaces are renting for, particularly if asked why the business is not willing to pay a certain price per square foot for the term of the lease.

Some business owners have the misconcep-

tion that negotiating for a better deal may upset a potential lender or landlord. This is untrue because good negotiation demonstrates understanding and concern for your finances. When concessions are not part of the negotiation, it may have the reverse effect of making the lender or landlord nervous. This can be especially true with lenders who may get the impression that a person is desperate for help. Also, it is best to ask a lot of questions of the other party to make sure you are aware of all the options. For instance, if you do not know what the interest rates and closing costs on all categories of loan options are, you may end up settling for a higher-priced loan. Often this type of information is not volunteered to an applicant.

> *When concessions are not part of the negotiation, it may have the reverse effect of making the lender or landlord nervous.*
>
> ———
>
> *It is best to begin negotiations with the most important points, and give any concessions on the lesser ones.*

Beginning negotiations are "first impressions" which should be made to stand out in the mind of the other party. Initial business meetings of any kind should be as diplomatic as possible because you are building a foundation for a serious matter. It is best to begin negotiations with the most important points and give any concessions on the lesser ones. In the case of a loan negotiation, the most important point may be the rate of interest or the term (duration) of the loan. In the case of a lease, the most important point may be the price per foot or the improvements that a landlord is willing to make at his expense. Whatever the case may be, by securing the most important issue first, you can be more flexible on the other points of the negotiation. As time goes on, if close attention is paid to the process, you will develop a "style" of negotiation that will make this part of business more comfortable, and sometimes even fun.

INVESTORS

Often a business owner will elect to seek capital from investors as opposed to placing the business in debt by originating a loan. In business there are two basic forms of investors: active investors and silent investors. Both types will become shareholders in the business in one way or another. Investors are in essence "partners" in the business (or aspect of the business) they have invested in. What distinguishes investors from lenders is the fact that they are willing to share the risk of the particular business endeavor. If the result of the investment is a profit, investors will share the profit and also keep their "financial position" in the business. On the other hand, if the result of the investment is a loss, investors will not realize a profit and may forfeit their original investment if the business does not survive.

A wise business owner will anticipate the future of the business before deciding between an investor or lender when working capital is needed. If the business capital is needed only as a "bridge" for a short period of time, a lender might be a smart choice. On the other hand, if the capital is needed for a long time period (more than three years), an investor may be the better choice. Often this financial decision may have to be made on the merits of an investor. If the investor is bringing needed expertise to the venture, this added asset may mean the difference in seeking the working capital or not. For example, if

> *A wise business owner will anticipate the future of the business before deciding between an investor or lender when working capital is needed.*

a business owner is thinking about expanding a product line to include an item that is unfamiliar, it may be wise to seek an investor who has experience in producing the new product. By doing this, the business owner gains the needed expertise and at the same time acquires the necessary capital for the project.

As a rule, when an investor contributes capital to a business, the amount of acquired capital relative to the value of the business will determine the investor's "share" in that business. For example, if the appraised value of a business is $100,000 after an investor contribution of $20,000, the investor would have a one-fifth share (or equity position) in that business. This rule does not always apply because a different agreement could be made prior to the investor's contribution. In other words, the investment process can be open to negotiation between all involved parties. These investment negotiations can deal with issues such as:

Terms of Investment

Duration of the Investment—The investment can be designed to terminate at the will of the business owner if the investment is paid back according to the agreement.

Business Share—Regardless of the market value of the business at the time of the investment, an agreement can be made that will assign a certain business share for that investment.

Specific Investment—An investor can contribute capital for only a specific product or business aspect which will be developed or produced with the help of the investment.

Position of the Investor—An investor can be either silent or active in the business he is investing in.

Liability of the Investor—If an investor does not wish to be a formal partner in the business, an agreement could be made which excludes the investor from the liability of the business.

Business capital can also be acquired by using a combination of investor capital and lender capital. This approach is sometimes taken when large amounts of capital (relative to the value of the business) are needed for expansion or retooling. Sometimes investor capital (and expertise) is needed for collateral when seeking a large business loan. This situation is referred to as a "wrap," and is designed to combine investor and lender capital. For example, if $150,000 is needed for expanding a business which is valued at $100,000 in assets, there would not be enough collateral to acquire the loan. If, however, an investor contributes $50,000 *cash* to the business prior to the signing of the loan, the necessary collateral would be in place, and only $100,000 would have to be borrowed from a lender.

LEVERAGING ASSETS

Once a business is up and running and has established a track record for loan repayment, some property assets may be acquired. The leveraging of assets, which is an increased means of accomplishing a goal, is how big financial leaps in business are often made. Leveraging is a form of equity financing in that it commits business property as collateral. This type of commitment does not relinquish a portion of the business to a shareholder or partner, and once repaid, the collateral property will be freed as it was before the lien existed. Ownership of the property is retained at

all times unless there is a default by the borrowing entity. For example, if a first or second deed of trust (lien) taken on a piece of property was used to acquire capital for a down payment on a second business location, additional capital may not be needed. In that case, the loan payment on the money borrowed could be paid each month by using the cash flow of the second (new) location. While paying the monthly debt service on the loan used for a down payment, additional business assets of the second location would be realized. If the business continues to flourish in both locations, these properties could then be used to repeat the leveraging process for further growth.

> *The leveraging of business assets is only beneficial when the potential gain far outweighs the cost of the loan.*

Equity share, which is the portion of property that is controlled , is the key to any financial leveraging. The leveraging of business assets is only beneficial when the potential gain far outweighs the cost of the loan. The *terms of the loan* (payment schedule) and *timing* of the acquisition (or need for capital) are both important considerations when the leveraging of business assets is considered. This timing includes the repayment schedule of the loan versus the rate of return at which the acquired asset (or accomplished goal) will yield. For instance, if $10,000 was borrowed to purchase a piece of property that increased in assessed value by that same amount, or produced a profit within a short amount of time (one year), the loan could then be paid off at very little cost. The same principle would apply to the acquisition of a piece of equipment that could produce a profit equal to the leveraged amount in a short time period.

VENDOR TERM ACCOUNTS

A vendor is a person or entity that *vends* or sells goods. For a woodworking business this would include all material suppliers, hardware suppliers and equipment suppliers that cater to it at the wholesale level. These business concerns sell us the necessary ingredients required to produce our products. When a business purchases from a supplier, price discounting or wholesale buying is an important issue to the buyer. The keys to profitability in the wholesale supply business are volume and a quick turnover of goods. Vendors do not usually operate on high profit percentages so they rely on quantity sales and a quick return on their investments. They also have fewer customers than the retail sales level, and should provide more personal service to their customers. It is always wise to investigate "price break" quantity thresholds with different vendors of the same product. It is common for suppliers to vary on this issue, and often money can be saved with just a little research. For instance, if two suppliers offer oak lumber (same quality) at the same price per board foot but have different wholesale prices when footage quantities are purchased, you can save money for your company with one phone call (see "Price Break Thresholds," page 29).

Wholesale suppliers have two basic catego-

ries of customer accounts: the cash account (C.O.D.) and the term account. Cash accounts are usually set up for new customers who do not have a track record with the supplier or for customers who simply elect to pay as they go. Term accounts are set up for frequent consumers as a convenience to all concerned. For example, if a business is buying a quantity of materials at least once a week, a term account would make it easier to keep a record of the transactions, and money would not have to change hands each time a delivery is made. The account would be settled as per the conditions set up by the vendor and consumer. Most term accounts are settled on a monthly basis usually by the tenth of each month, but can be paid off or "carried" according to what has been prearranged.

Vendor term accounts usually include an added benefit for the wholesale consumers. An additional discount, which is over and above any volume or wholesale discount, is sometimes allowed if the account is paid by a predetermined date. This discount is usually about 2 percent of the net amount of the order, and is designed as an added incentive for the customer to settle the account promptly. These "early pay" discounts are sometimes offered to term account customers automatically and other times must be negotiated. The consuming business owner should always request that a discount be provided for settling vendor accounts earlier than is stated in the terms of the account. For example, if the net amount of a material order was $1,000 and the terms of the account called for full payment in 30 days, a 2 percent discount for settling the account in 15 days would equate to $20.

As time goes on and a vendor gets to know you and your business, credit limits can be increased or the terms of the account can be modified to accommodate you. For instance, if you have used a supplier for the past four years and

> *When a business purchases from a supplier, price discounting or wholesale buying is an important issue to the buyer.*
>
> ---
>
> *It is always wise to investigate "price break" quantity thresholds with different vendors of the same product.*

COMPANY A		COMPANY B		COMPANY C	
F.A.S. Red Oak		**F.A.S. Red Oak**		**F.A.S. Red Oak**	
100-250 B.F.	= $3.00 B.F.	100-200 B.F.	= $3.00 B.F.	100-500 B.F.	= $3.00 B.F.
250-500 B.F.	= $2.75 B.F.	200-500 B.F.	= $2.75 B.F.	500-750 B.F.	= $2.75 B.F.
500-1000 B.F.	= $2.50 B.F.	500-750 B.F.	= $2.50 B.F.	750-1000 B.F.	= $2.50 B.F.
over 1000 B.F.	= $2.25 B.F.	over 750 B.F.	= $2.25 B.F.	over 1000 B.F.	= $2.25 B.F.
F.A.S. Domestic Walnut		**F.A.S. Domestic Walnut**		**F.A.S. Domestic Walnut**	
100-250 B.F.	= $4.25 B.F.	100-200 B.F.	= $4.25 B.F.	100-500 B.F.	= $4.25 B.F.
250-500 B.F.	= $4.05 B.F.	200-500 B.F.	= $4.05 B.F.	500-750 B.F.	= $4.05 B.F.
500-1000 B.F.	= $3.75 B.F.	500-750 B.F.	= $3.75 B.F.	750-1000 B.F.	= $3.75 B.F.
over 1000 B.F.	= $3.50 B.F.	over 750 B.F.	= $3.50 B.F.	over 1000 B.F.	= $3.50 B.F.
F.A.S. Honduras Mahongany		**F.A.S. Honduras Mahongany**		**F.A.S. Honduras Mahongany**	
100-250 B.F.	= $5.25 B.F.	100-200 B.F.	= $5.25 B.F.	100-500 B.F.	= $5.25 B.F.
250-500 B.F.	= $5.05 B.F.	200-500 B.F.	= $5.05 B.F.	500-750 B.F.	= $5.05 B.F.
500-1000 B.F.	= $4.75 B.F.	500-750 B.F.	= $4.75 B.F.	750-1000 B.F.	= $4.75 B.F.
over 1000 B.F.	= $4.50 B.F.	over 750 B.F.	= $4.50 B.F.	over 1000 B.F.	= $4.50 B.F.

It is common for suppliers to vary on the issue of price break "thresholds" for quantity wholesale buying. Money can often be saved by comparing vendors and quantity thresholds.

a situation arises where you will need to increase your credit line, a phone call to that vendor will usually be sufficient to increase the line. The vendor will usually look at your payment history with his company and make a decision promptly. Once the credit line has been increased, it will normally stay at the new level unless the vendor specifies otherwise. Increased credit lines with suppliers are also desirable when credit applications to other entities (lenders, suppliers, lines of credit) are submitted. Each time a business is looked upon favorably by an increase in a credit line, it is recorded and taken into account by all other business suppliers.

EMPLOYEE CONCERNS

Employers must adhere to many obligations under federal tax laws (Internal Revenue Service) and labor laws (Department of Labor). The decision to be an employer will impact a business in many ways. First and foremost, there will be an added function in the accounting aspect of the business. Some of the issues which are handled by accounting include:

Federal and State Payroll Withholdings

This is money which is held out of an employee's base pay for income tax and Social Security

> *The consuming business owner should always request that a discount be provided for settling vendor accounts earlier than is stated in the terms of the account.*

> *Each time a business is looked upon favorably by an increase in a credit line, it is recorded and taken into account by all other business suppliers.*
>
> ———
>
> *Employers should have a separate checking account for deposit of employee withholdings until the money is actually paid to the respective agencies.*

payments, and is paid to the respective agencies on a monthly or quarterly basis. Employers should have a separate checking account for deposit of employee withholdings until the money is actually paid to the respective agencies.

Unemployment Insurance

This money is collected partly from employee withholdings and is coupled with payments directly from the employer. It will be paid as unemployment insurance for employees in the event they are laid off or fired until they find a new position.

Workers' Compensation Insurance

This is paid by the employer as insurance in the event of a disabling accident while an employee is working for the business. Workers' comp can be paid monthly or quarterly.

Benefit Payments

Any benefits which are part of an employee pay package, such as retirement programs and medi-cal insurance, must be paid or put in escrow in a timely manner for the employee.

Payroll

Employee payroll is usually paid on a weekly, biweekly or monthly basis. After all payroll withholdings are calculated, checks must be issued at the end of each pay period.

Record Keeping

There are records which must be kept on at least a weekly basis which document any employee payments, transaction or scheduling.

It is always best to confer with a good business accountant regarding all the above-mentioned employee concerns before establishing your company's policies regarding employees. A business accountant can also inform an employer about laws which are mandated by the Department of Labor, and any benefits which might be gained by employing on a part-time basis as opposed to full-time. Part-time work is anything under forty hours a week and can be a combination of full or partial shifts. Key employees are usually employed as "full-time workers," and as a result are entitled to any benefits which are set up by the company.

EMPLOYEE CODES OF CONDUCT

Whenever potential employees are selected, and before they are actually hired, a code of ethics should be supplied by the business and accepted by the employees. This company code of ethics should be designed to anticipate any questions or likely situations that could be uncomfortable for the employer. Employee codes of conduct are guidelines stating what the company will allow or prohibit. In other words, these are basically company rules and regulations which must be presented to potential employees before they are hired. Some common business conduct concerns would include:

Fiduciary Responsibilities

Establish a policy for giving gifts to or receiving gifts from clients or suppliers.

Confidentiality of Business Information

Organizational information should not be used for personal gain by an employee or to harm the business as a whole.

> *It is always best to confer with a good business accountant regarding employee concerns before establishing your company's policies regarding employees.*

Conflict of Interest

Employees must avoid any situations where there is a financial or personal conflict between the organization and the employee.

Misuse of Organizational Position

A clear definition should be given as to what would constitute misuse of position when dealing with vendors, fellow employees, clientele or business competitors.

Substance Abuse

A clear mandate must be given regarding abuse of both legal and illegal substances.

Ethics

A clear statement should define what is ethical and what is not.

Equal Employment Opportunity

Requirements and prohibitions should be explained regarding what employees should know if they were in a position of hiring or firing another employee.

Sexual Harassment

A clear mandate should spell out sexual harassment policies.

Organizational Facilities Usage

A list of restrictions should be presented regarding private or off-duty use of business facilities.

Relationships Between Employees

Any specific mandates which cover personal relationships between employees should be stated.

CHAPTER SUMMARY

- Lack of financial knowledge is an understandable reason for making a person think twice about entering into business. What is really needed is fundamental knowledge of finances and how they work, a good accountant, and some direction for finding the right answers. Building business assets while regular operations are continuing is how a business will grow. Local banks and lending institutions can provide information about specific lending programs. The Small Business Administration can be contacted as a resource for answers to many financial and tax questions regarding a new or existing business.

- Because they are in business, formal lenders will structure their loans so that the return on money invested is equal to or greater than the risk factors involved. There are many factors which make up the risk equation in the eyes of a lender. The amount of collateral that a business owner is willing to pledge directly affects the motivation to repay the loan in the eyes of a lender. Lenders will adjust the committed security according to its liquidity. The liquid value of the collateral will affect the interest rate and approval of a loan. There are many banks to choose from, some of which are more familiar with a specific industry or which may assess your business situation differently.

- Before serious business growth can take place, space and capital will be needed. Bank loans are the traditional means by which working capital is obtained. Lines of credit are easier to access than bank loans, but are usually due each year in one lump sum. Loans for a new business are much more difficult to obtain than they are for an established business. Regardless of the business circumstance, the loan process is always the same. A loan application must be submitted with current financial information about the business or business owner's personal assets. There must also be a specific plan for both the use of the money and the means by which it will be paid back.

- Depending upon the business, there is a particular type of financing which most benefits it. Each time a financial commitment is resolved per the terms of the agreement a favorable rating will be entered into the business's credit history.

- The primary goal of the Small Business Administration (SBA) is to help small business owners start and build a strong business. Small business employs 50 percent of the private work force in the United States, and generates more than 50 percent of the gross domestic product. The SBA has a Web site, as well as offices in every state which can be contacted for personal service and advice.

- The decisions that are made during important financial negotiations may have to be lived with for a long time. All negotiations are a process of give and take and the agreement outcome will favor the best negotiator. A person who is best prepared with current and correct information will have an edge in any negotiation.

- A prepared negotiator will try to anticipate the questions that may be asked and have a preplanned response to those questions.

- Business owners will sometimes seek capital from investors as opposed to placing the business in debt by originating a loan. Investors are in essence "partners" in the business which they have invested in. If the investor is bringing needed expertise to the venture, this added asset may affect the decision to seek working capital or not.

- Business capital can also be acquired by using a combination of investor capital and lender capital.

- Leveraging is a form of equity financing in that it commits business property as collateral. Ownership of the leveraged property is retained at all times unless there is a default by the borrowing entity. Equity share is the key to any financial leveraging.

- Woodworking business vendors include: material suppliers, hardware suppliers and equipment suppliers. Vendors do not usually operate on high profit percentages, so they are relying upon quantity sales and a quick return on their investments. It is common for suppliers to vary on the issue of price break thresholds. Vendor term accounts make it easier to keep a record of transactions, and money does not have to change hands each time a delivery is made. With vendor term accounts, an additional discount can sometimes be taken for paying off the account early. After a vendor knows your company, credit limits may be increased or the terms of the account can be modified to accommodate you.

- As an employer, there are many obligations under federal tax and labor laws that must be adhered to. Some of the issues which will be handled by the accounting department include: federal and state payroll withholdings, unemployment insurance, Workers' Compensation insurance, benefit payments, payroll and record keeping. A business accountant can also inform an employer about laws mandated by the Department of Labor and any benefits that can be gained by employing on a part-time basis.

- A code of conduct should be supplied by an employer and accepted by potential employees before they are hired. Employee codes of conduct are guidelines as to what the company will allow or prohibit. Some common business conduct concerns include: fiduciary responsibilities, confidentiality of business information, conflict of interest, misuse of organizational position, substance abuse, ethics, Equal Employment Opportunity, sexual harassment, organizational facilities usage and relationships between employees.

4

Estimating, Bidding and Pricing Your Work

One of the first questions I'm asked in my furniture building classes and seminars is "How do you estimate and price your work?" Of course there are a lot of variables in the many different products and markets in the woodworking world, but believe it or not, there is a formula that can be applied in all cases. Although I have worked in all the woodworking categories, I am presently involved in the one-of-a-kind (or custom) market. I believe this is the most difficult category to estimate. The estimating formula which follows, however, has served me well through the years and will work for any type of woodworking business that produces a product.

The four basic parts of this equation, overhead, labor costs, materials, and profit, must be examined, analyzed and scrutinized individually. Overhead will be calculated on a per-day basis, and labor will be calculated on a per-hour basis. Materials are what they are, and profit is simply a percentage which is added on to the total of overhead, labor and materials (O, L and M). Along with this bidding formula a certain amount of planning and analysis must be conducted in advance of bidding. In other words, the project to be bid must be properly defined. I have always found this investment of time to be well worth the effort even if I do not get the job.

Among other things, this chapter will break down in detail my bidding formula and how it should work. Keep in mind that we all have made

or will make pricing mistakes along the way, but one cannot habitually lose money and expect to survive in business. Losses can be prevented by learning from our own mistakes as well as the mistakes of others where pricing and bidding are concerned. While paying attention to your own past bidding mistakes, you can also keep a careful eye on the competition. Do not be ashamed to ask associates or colleagues how they would handle certain bidding situations. Often ideas can be shared that will keep you from making the same mistake that was made by someone else. My formula is a basic framework which can be altered or elaborated upon depending on the complexity of the particular business. For example, the one-man shop would not have the same profit structure or employee costs as a large corporation.

DEFINING OVERHEAD

The first part of my bidding formula has to do with overhead, or general business costs. Overhead is defined as *the general, continuing costs involved in running a business*. These include rent, furnishings, equipment payments or leases, utilities, taxes, insurance, office expenses, etc. In other words, any money that must be spent on a continual basis (weekly, monthly, yearly) to keep a business operating is considered to be part of general overhead. All costs within this category must be considered and added to the total if they

Overhead (per day) **+** Labor (per hour) **+**

Materials (everything) **+** Profit (15%–20%) **=**

PRICE

There are four basic components that make up the bidding formula: overhead, labor, materials and profit. This pricing formula should work for any woodworking business.

are part of general overhead. This is very important and costs can be ever changing. A periodic evaluation of overhead costs can only help insure that this important part of the pricing formula is accurate. We have all heard the advice, "Keep your overhead down." This is important because, as you will see, overhead is factored into the price of our work. If our overhead becomes too great, we will price ourselves out of the market. For example, a shop that is operating with equipment that it owns will be able to underbid a shop that is operating with expensive equipment that is leased or financed.

Once these continual costs of overhead are added up on a monthly basis, a per-day dollar amount can be calculated (see "Monthly Overhead Expenses," p. 36). This is simple to do and all-important to the bidding formula. If you know what it costs per day to operate your business, it is easy to calculate how much of that daily cost should be paid by a particular client. One important thing to consider when calculating the per-day costs of overhead is the amount of hours a day and days per week your business will/does operate. For instance, my business (at least theoretically) operates five eight-hour days per week for business purposes. With that in mind, if my monthly overhead is $1,000, then my general overhead will cost me $50 a day ($1,000 for twenty eight-hour days per month). By figuring my overhead this way, the entire month's general costs will be paid by clientele with approximately 160 hours of work per month (40 hours a week). As for the rest of the hours in the month, I can do what I please in the shop. For example, if I care to build a speculative piece of furniture or something for myself after work or on Saturday, the cost of shop time is not an issue.

DEFINING LABOR

The second part of my formula deals with labor, which is defined as *any physical or mental exertion or work*. With that definition in mind, any physical or mental exertion that will be spent on

a client's project should be considered when estimating a project's labor cost. In other words, labor for a specific project not only includes the time that it takes to actually produce the work, but also the time spent thinking, drawing and meeting with the client. Without a lot of experience, mental exertion is probably the most difficult aspect of labor to calculate, but it must be taken into consideration. I have had clients who simply could not make up their mind during the critical planning stage of a project and, consequently, used up my entire labor budget for the project in the process. Other clients will leave a lot of the detail up to me, the builder, which will render the mental part of the labor less of a concern.

We all know that each client will be different from another. If your business is strictly custom or commissioned work, the clientele contact is likely to be a little more time consuming than for an "ongoing production" client. The client's personality is also very important. Your opinion about your potential client's personality can be formed early in the initial meeting stages. Without getting into a lot of psychology, the only thing I can offer here is to be as observant as possible when first courting a client. Do they return calls promptly? Are they on time for your meetings? Do they get right to the point when asked a question, or do they ramble on? Do they seem to know what they want before you talk to them, or are they vague? Little things like these can tell you a lot about how your future dealings will go with that client. Of course, all relationships are devel-

MONTHLY OVERHEAD EXPENSES

RENT, LEASE OR OWN PAYMENT:	
EQUIPMENT PAYMENTS:	
POWER:	
WATER:	
HEATING:	
TAXES:	
INSURANCE:	
OFFICE EXPENSES:	
MONTHLY TOTAL:	
DIVIDED BY THE NUMBER OF DAYS OF OPERATION:	
OVERHEAD COST PER DAY:	

For bidding purposes, overhead, which is the monthly cost of doing business, should be calculated and converted into a cost *per day*.

oped between the individuals involved, so basic honesty is the most important thing to pay attention to.

ESTIMATING TIME

Estimating the time it takes to do the actual work will become easier with experience. In the meantime, always figure that if something can go wrong, it will (Murphy's Law), and be realistic about your capabilities. Again, you do not want to price yourself out of the market, but you do not want to work for free either. There is a balance between efficiency (the optimum time it takes to do a given job) and the rate of pay one can earn. If you are learning on someone's job, you cannot expect to charge them for all the hours you spend trying new techniques or the consultation time you spend with another craftsperson. Even when one is experienced at estimating hours, a 5 percent margin should be added to the total for all the unexpected problems that may arise. For example, if you feel that something is going to take you 100 hours to complete, add 5 percent for a total bid of 105 hours.

LABOR

When figuring labor costs for the purposes of a bid, a total of all hours spent on a project must be considered. This will include both what you pay yourself and what you pay your employees who will work on that job. For the employees' time, this would be a gross amount per hour that includes their actual wage and all other expenses associated with that wage. The extra employee expenses include things like liability insurance, matching Social Security payments, unemployment insurance, etc., which must be paid by the business. We all have to pay the same federal expenses for employees, but state costs for them do vary. As an average, employees usually cost about one and one-half times the hourly wage

You do not want to price yourself out of the market, but you do not want to work for free either.

——————

When figuring labor costs for the purposes of a bid, a total of all hours spent on a project must be considered.

they are paid. So if you are paying someone ten dollars an hour, that person is really costing you fifteen dollars an hour.

Somewhat the same principle also applies to the owner/operator. Regardless of how you are paying yourself, a weekly salary or a per-hour rate, any related employment costs will have to be considered. If you would like to net a specific hourly wage for the hours you work, the related costs should be added to that wage for bidding purposes. This hourly rate will be the same for all aspects of the job. Remember, the labor factor is your income, and that is what you will live on and invest.

WHAT SHOULD I CHARGE FOR MY WORK?

Invariably I am asked the question "What should I charge per hour for my work?" and I always answer with the question "What do you think your time is worth?" We all have some sort of opinion regarding what we would like to make per hour. This opinion coupled with some realism can help you arrive at an hourly wage that is in keeping with the competition and acceptable to you. Before deciding what you would like your wage to be, keep the business itself in mind. When starting a new business, your wage should grow naturally if the business itself is built on a good foundation. In other words, you might have to settle for less money per hour in the beginning in order to keep the jobs coming. With this approach a new business can grow steadily. Good cash flow is important for a business to survive!

Hourly Wages

Hourly wages are based upon several variables. Education, knowledge of the subject, craftsmanship and experience are some personal attributes. Market demographics and marketability of a product also affect wages. If you have experience in the woodworking category before starting a business of that type (which is always a good idea), you should already know what to charge for your time. If the new business is related to your experience, but not necessarily what you are used to, then you will have to do some research before determining your hourly rate. Before beginning a business or producing a new product that you are unsure of, check out the competition in that field. If there is no competition locally, look toward the closest big city or comparable market. See what another business in your area would charge for a similar type of product. This information from a competitor will help you decide if you can compete at the wage you desire within that geographic area.

> *When starting a new business, your wage should grow naturally if the business itself is built on a good foundation.*
>
> ---
>
> *Before beginning a business or producing a new product that you are unsure of, check out the competition in that field.*

SALARY

A salary is a *fixed* payment at regular intervals for services. In the woodworking industry, salaries are usually paid to the hierarchy of a company or corporation. Anyone from the owner/operator of a sole proprietorship to the CEO of a corporation can be compensated by salary. Salaries may also be paid to key employees such as managers and superintendents who are responsible for an important aspect of a business. Some people prefer a salary to an hourly wage even if they don't get paid for overtime. With a salary you are paid rain or shine, and the "efforts vs. salary" ratio should all average out in the long run. In other words, if you get sick one day or business is slow for a month, you are still paid your salary, and this should make up for the overtime that is needed at times of peak demand.

A salary can be structured in many different ways. It can be calculated monthly, yearly or for any specific predetermined time, but is usually paid weekly, biweekly or monthly. Some companies may decide to pay salaries on a biweekly or monthly basis because it is cheaper than weekly for clerical and accounting reasons. Salaries can also be designed to include a combination of dollar amount, company stock and a host of other compensation benefits. Income taxes will have to be paid on the total value of the compensation at the time that it is dispersed. It is a good idea to have a tax consultant review your salary plans before they are implemented.

The decision to pay yourself or a key employee a salary is based on several factors. In a corporate structure, a salary is usually paid to management personnel, as opposed to the labor force. Salary *positions* themselves are evaluated, not individuals, and there is a reasonable range within which to work. A job evaluation system will rank each position based on knowledge required, decision-making responsibilities and impact on a corporation. A clearly defined procedure for performance reviews will yield salary increases to the most deserving and will be coupled with "cost of living" increases. In all other forms of business entity, salaries are usually paid according to seniority and position impact. This means that if a person has been with the company for a period of time (with a good track record) and is considered to be a key employee, a salary may be more desirable.

Where the company or corporation itself is concerned, there are other factors which will have to be weighed before a salary is paid. First and foremost of these factors is the position in question. If the key position is long-term and is expected to be an ongoing part of the business, it may be wise to pay a salary to the right person

> *Materials and supplies should always be charged to your customer at "retail" regardless of the price level at which they were purchased.*

in order to keep him "comfortable" and secure with the job. Remember a person on salary gets paid the same regardless of the amount of time spent on the job. There is a slight additional cost in calculating the tax and withholding amounts for wage positions. While a salaried position will withhold the same amount each pay period, the withholdings must be calculated each pay period for a wage position. This cost is usually offset by the fact that wage positions are less compensatory than salaried positions.

MATERIAL, SUPPLIES AND WOOD AS A COMMODITY

The third part of the bidding equation is the material and supply costs of the project to be bid. This is much easier to calculate than the general overhead or the hours required to do a project. Materials and supplies should always be charged to your customer at "retail" regardless of the price level at which they were purchased. The privilege of paying wholesale is offset by all the logistics involved in being in business. State and local business licenses, the accounting we need to do, storage facilities for our materials and minimum quantities required by vendors are just a few of the reasons that we are allowed to buy at wholesale.

Once a project has been broken down into its various components, prices can be calculated and added up to a total (see "Project Material and

PROJECT MATERIAL AND SUPPLY COSTS

EXAMPLE: 6' WIDE WALNUT HUTCH/BUFFET WITH GLASS UPPER DOORS	
125 BD.FT. OF 4/4 BLACK WALNUT @$4.25 A BD.FT. (FOR PRIMARY CASEWORK)	
16 BD.FT. OF 4/4 ALDER (FOR CLEATS, STRONGBACKS, ETC.)	
1.5 SHEETS OF ¾" WALNUT PLYWOOD @$2.50 A SQ.FT. (FOR BOTTOMS, TOP OF UPPER, DIVISIONS)	
1.5 SHEETS OF ¼" WALNUT PLYWOOD @$1.75 A SQ.FT. (FOR CABINET BACKS)	
8 SQ.FT. OF DOUBLE STRENGTH CLEAR GLASS (FOR UPPER CABINET DOORS)	
SUPPLIES (NAILS, GLUE, SANDPAPER, SCREWS)	
HARDWARE (DRAWER SLIDES, HINGES, DOOR AND DRAWER PULLS, DOOR CATCHES)	
FINISHING PRODUCTS (STAIN, VARNISH, BRUSHES, RAGS, STEELWOOL, WAX)	
SUBTOTAL:	
SALES TAX (IF APPLICABLE):	
TOTAL:	

When figuring the material and supplies that will be necessary to complete a project, everything involved in a project should be considered.

Supply Costs," p. 39). As I mention in my furniture classes, *everything* that goes into a project must be considered. Not that you have to estimate every nail and screw, but all materials and supplies should be thought of and somehow averaged in. The sandpaper, glue, fasteners, stain, finishes, etc. are all things that we need to purchase and are important parts of our projects. I will usually add 5 percent of the total material (lumber and plywood) costs to my estimate. This percentage will cover the costs of the "extraneous" supplies that are necessary for the job.

FACTORING IN LUMBER

Where lumber is concerned, there is a "downfall," or waste factor, which varies according to the grade of material purchased. Hardwood that is graded as FAS (firsts and seconds) material will have far less waste than say #2 or #3 common. Regardless of the grade of lumber that is actually used, a retail price for the grade that will most resemble the finished look should be used. Example: If a project is to be "stain grade" as opposed to "paint grade," then a better grade of material would be necessary.

When FAS is used, the actual board footages puchased for a project will usually total 10 to 15 percent more than the finished product square footages. This percentage should be added into the material list. Waste such as knots, splits, checks, saw kerf, etc. account for this percentage. Remember, the grade of lumber we use is a matter of preference, but you can't justify charging someone 50 percent waste unless the material is specified by the client to be a lower grade.

The commodity aspect of wood has to do with how and when we buy. Unless you are buying warehouses full of lumber, the word "commodity" has little to do with prices going up or down. That concept doesn't really seem to apply to lumber "users" in that the prices just seem to

If lumber is purchased in the rough state, the milling charges will be saved.

go up. Making money on our material is more a matter of the quantities we purchase and the brackets (or thresholds) that are crossed during quantity buying. In wholesale buying, suppliers will offer better prices when larger quantities are purchased. For instance, there are usually price breaks for 100–500 bf, and then again for 500–1000 bf, and so on. The prices that are paid for material can really affect the bottom line of a business. For instance, if FAS oak is $4.50 a board foot retail, and you can buy 500 to 1,000 board feet at under $2.00 a board foot, you will make more than $2.50 a board foot on the material itself. Of course this is a matter of whether or not you can use 500 or 1,000 feet in a reasonable amount of time and you are not paying premium prices for storage space. It is a balancing act, but well worth some thought and planning.

Another important consideration regarding lumber as a commodity is the way in which we specify the order. If we order our material surfaced (S2S) and straight-lined (S3S), there will be milling charges added to the price. If lumber is purchased in the rough state, the milling charges will be saved. I have always gotten a kick out of the fact that it costs me more money to realize less wood when I have the lumber mill surface and edge my lumber. I personally prefer to dress my own lumber for several reasons. By purchasing the lumber rough, I am saving approximately ten cents per foot, but I also have the privilege of getting all the wood I've paid for. On the technical end, and money aside, we all know that rough lumber is not always flat and straight. At the mill the material is simply sent through the planer and comes out just as crooked as it went in (only less thick). I prefer to run one face of my lumber over the jointer before I send it through the planer to take out any of the warping or twisting that might be present. Another good reason to buy lumber rough is that it affords the ability to "resaw." In any event, money can always be saved by dressing your own lumber. Dressing your own lumber will afford you more technical and quality control.

DEFINING PROFIT

The final part of my bidding formula has to do with the word *profit* which is defined as *financial or monetary gain from the use of capital in a transaction or series of transactions*. Profit is something that every business needs in order to survive. The percentage of profit that a business makes is the ratio of capital invested to the actual selling price of the product. Remember that profit is separate from overhead, labor and materials, and is quite simply a percentage which is added onto the total cost of these three things (see "Figuring Profit" below). For the woodworking industry, 15 to 20 percent is usually the average profit margin.

Among other things, profit is what keeps a business growing and up-to-date. Purchase of better and more specific tools, product development, advertising, maintenance and physical

> *Profit is what keeps a business growing and up-to-date.*

expansion are just a few things that should be paid for by profits. These things should not come out of your salary or borrowed money if it can be helped. In a corporate structure, profit is also used to pay stockholders their annual dividends, according to how the board of directors decides.

In business, other strengths are realized from actual profits. As years go by and a good track record for profit is established, a company's credit rating will increase—that is, if the company pays its bills. Regardless of how a company uses its profits, the fact that it is making money looks good to banks, vendors and lending institutions. When a business approaches a bank, vendor or lending institution for credit of any kind, the first thing that is asked for is a copy of the Profit and Loss (P&L) statement for that business. The creditor will usually want to see a current P&L, and often would like to see a three-year history. Even the biggest companies experience bad quarters, but when applying for credit the general trend should be a profit, not a loss.

Reinvesting Profit

As explained earlier, profits are the most important part of any ongoing successful business. Every business entity has its own idea of how the profit should be distributed. A smart company or corporation will reinvest at least part of its profits on a regular basis. If profits are reinvested wisely, a compounding effect should be the natural result. As mentioned earlier, new and better tools, advertising, product development, quantity buying and physical expansion are all good ways of reinvesting profit. The reduction of debt is another way of leveraging business profit. If, for

FIGURING PROFIT

Overhead cost @ $75 per day × 3 days	$225
Labor costs @ $15 per hour × 24 hours	$360
Materials used	$140
SUBTOTAL:	$725
16 percent profit × subtotal (.16 × $725)	$116
TOTAL COST:	$841

Profit is what enables a business to survive and grow. The percentage of profit is added to the total cost of overhead, labor and materials.

instance, you have a business loan at 12 percent interest per year, it may be wise to reduce or resolve the loan and keep the 12 percent. This would also free up the credit line as well as reduce the general overhead which will translate into more profit.

> *If profits are reinvested wisely, a compounding effect should be the natural result.*

TIME AND MATERIALS

The term *time and materials*, or T&M, is often associated with construction projects. This is not the normal way of bidding on a project, but sometimes, when there is trust involved, this might be the best way of attacking the unknown. Simply put, T&M means that a client will pay for the project materials (directly or indirectly) and any time or expense that a person or company spends to do the work. The drawbacks are evident for the client. This approach renders the project "open ended" in terms of the costs. For the contractor, it is a comfortable position to be in, but honesty and accountability are very important.

I have had many situations in my career where T&M was the only way I would consider a project, especially when asked to restore the woodworking and interior of a historic building. In those cases, there is no way of knowing the total involvement until after the project is in progress. True, the majority of the work can be estimated, but until foundational walls can be examined, there is no way of knowing what will have to be restored. Other variables may also dictate how a project is considered. Regional weather, specific material availability, a client's budget (which may cause a project to stop and start) and

the local labor force are just a few of these variables. It is hard to produce a profit if you do not know exactly what you are bidding on, so consider your approach carefully.

Other ways that a time and materials approach can be used are: T&M is not to exceed a certain dollar amount or bidding on the known aspects of a project and T&M is specified on the unknown aspects. Both of these approaches will help make a client more comfortable with the process. The "T&M not to exceed" approach is commonly used when incremental budgeting is an issue. In other words, a client may have funds for a project at his disposal, but those funds are allocated over time for some reason or another. This is considered to be an ongoing project that will obviously lose some efficiency because of the stop-and-start scenario. It is hard to make a firm bid on a project when you cannot control the efficiency aspects. In the other case, bidding on the known portion with T&M on the unknown portion, some control can be realized by the client. If you can "hammer down" a majority of the project with a firm bid, the client will be more relaxed about the T&M on the unknowns.

CONTRACT PROPOSALS AND CONTRACTS

A contract proposal is a plan that is either denied, altered or agreed upon by the parties concerned. Unless it is denied somewhere along the line, a proposal will ultimately become a contract. I use proposals similar to the one shown here in my woodworking business (see "Sample Proposal" opposite). Proposals are quite helpful in negotiating the terms of the business at hand. Similar to real estate offers, there are always details to consider when refining the terms of the agreement. Price, timing, dimensions, choice of materials, deposit amounts and delivery are just some of the many concerns that might need to be discussed further before a proposal will turn into a contractual

P R O P O S A L

SAL MACCARONE
WOODWORK DESIGNER/CRAFTSMAN

4527 Mariposa Creek Circle
Mariposa, California 95338
(209) 966-4152/Fax (209) 966-6573

PROPOSAL SUBMITTED TO	PHONE	DATE
STREET	JOB NAME	
CITY, STATE AND ZIP CODE	JOB LOCATION	
ARCHITECT DATE OF PLANS	JOB PHONE	

WE HEREBY SUBMIT SPECIFICATIONS AND ESTIMATES FOR:

DESCRIPTION OF WORK:

MATERIAL TO BE USED:

FINISH TO BE USED:

HARDWARE TO BE USED:

DELIVERY DATE:

INSTALLATION:

WE PROPOSE TO HEREBY TO FURNISH MATERIAL AND LABOR—COMPLETE IN ACCORDANCE WITH
ABOVE SPECIFICATIONS, FOR THE SUM OF _____ DOLLARS ($ _____)

PAYMENT TO BE MADE AS FOLLOWS:

ALL MATERIAL IS GUARANTEED TO BE AS SPECIFIED. ALL WORK TO
BE COMPLETED IN A WORKMANLIKE MANNER ACCORDING TO
STANDARD PRACTICES. ANY ALTERATION OR DEVIATION FROM
ABOVE SPECIFICATIONS INVOLVING EXTRA COSTS WILL BE
EXECUTED ONLY UPON WRITTEN ORDERS, AND WILL BECOME AN
EXTRA CHARGE OVER AND ABOVE THE ESTIMATE. ALL AGREEMENTS
CONTINGENT UPON STRIKES, ACCIDENTS OR DELAYS BEYOND
OUR CONTROL. OWNER TO CARRY FIRE, TORNADO AND OTHER   AUTHORIZED SIGNATURE _____
NECESSARY INSURANCE. OUR WORKERS ARE FULLY COVERED BY   NOTE: THIS PROPOSAL MAY BE WITHDRAWN BY US
WORKMEN'S COMPENSATION INSURANCE.   IF NOT ACCEPTED WITHIN _____ DAYS.

ACCEPTANCE OF PROPOSAL

THE ABOVE PRICES, SPECIFICATIONS AND CONDITIONS ARE
SATISFACTORY AND ARE HEREBY ACCEPTED. YOU ARE AUTHORIZED
TO DO THE WORK AS SPECIFIED. PAYMENT WILL BE MADE AS
OUTLINED ABOVE.   SIGNATURE _____
DATE OF ACCEPTANCE _____   SIGNATURE _____

A proposal can be amended and refined. As you and the client work out the details of the project, the proposal will eventually evolve into a contract.

SAL MACCARONE

WOODWORK DESIGNER/CRAFTSMAN

4527 Mariposa Creek Circle

Mariposa, California 95338

(209) 966-4152/Fax (209) 966-6573

PROPOSAL SUBMITTED TO	PHONE	DATE
STREET	JOB NAME	
CITY, STATE AND ZIP CODE	JOB LOCATION	
ARCHITECT DATE OF PLANS	JOB PHONE	

WE HEREBY SUBMIT SPECIFICATIONS AND ESTIMATES FOR:

DESCRIPTION OF WORK:

MATERIAL TO BE USED:

FINISH TO BE USED:

HARDWARE TO BE USED:

DELIVERY DATE:

INSTALLATION:

WE WILL FURNISH MATERIAL AND LABOR—COMPLETE IN ACCORDANCE WITH ABOVE SPECIFICATIONS, FOR THE SUM OF _____ DOLLARS ($ _____)

ALL MATERIAL IS GUARANTEED TO BE AS SPECIFIED. ALL WORK TO BE COMPLETED IN A WORKMANLIKE MANNER ACCORDING TO STANDARD PRACTICES. ANY ALTERATION OR DEVIATION FROM ABOVE SPECIFICATIONS INVOLVING EXTRA COSTS WILL BE EXECUTED ONLY UPON WRITTEN ORDERS, AND WILL BECOME AN EXTRA CHARGE OVER AND ABOVE THE ESTIMATE. ALL AGREEMENTS CONTINGENT UPON STRIKES, ACCIDENTS OR DELAYS BEYOND OUR CONTROL. OWNER TO CARRY FIRE, TORNADO AND OTHER NECESSARY INSURANCE. OUR WORKERS ARE FULLY COVERED BY WORKMEN'S COMPENSATION INSURANCE.

AUTHORIZED SIGNATURE _____

ACCEPTANCE OF CONTRACT

THE ABOVE PRICES, SPECIFICATIONS AND CONDITIONS ARE SATISFACTORY AND ARE HEREBY ACCEPTED. YOU ARE AUTHORIZED TO DO THE WORK AS SPECIFIED. PAYMENT WILL BE MADE AS OUTLINED ABOVE.

SIGNATURE _____

DATE OF ACCEPTANCE _____

SIGNATURE _____

A written contract should include a description of the work to be done, the financial terms of the agreement, completion dates and any product disclaimers that might apply.

agreement. I look at proposals as "tools" that are used for producing good contracts (see "Sample Contract" on p. 44).

Simply put, a contract is an agreement (verbal or written) between two or more parties. Of course, a contract can be as simple as a handshake or as complex as necessary and still be legally binding. The handshake contract may be good when cutting a board for friends or relatives, but I would strongly recommend a *written* contract for any agreement with clients. Written contracts are not only more professional, but more importantly, there are no misunderstandings due to loss of memory. Everyone is more comfortable with a written contract when it comes to business.

> *Written contracts are not only more professional, but more importantly, there are no misunderstandings due to loss of memory.*
>
> *It is better to design a contract specific to your business; then you know what is in it.*

For my woodworking business, I have always believed that simplicity is the key when designing a contract. Beyond the basic information such as date, names, addresses and a description of the work, only the terms of the agreement and a place for the signatures need be provided. Form contracts are all right, but make sure that you read all the fine print yourself before signing it. I have known people to get themselves in a "wringer" by signing a form contract. It is better to design a contract specific to your business; then you know what is in it. Depending on the complexity of your business, you may or may not want to seek the advice of a business consultant or attorney as to the proper contract design for you.

NEGOTIATING A GOOD CONTRACT

A contract must work both ways! The contractor and the customer should be protected by the terms of the agreement. When I am designing a contract (while it is still in the proposal stage), I try to look at the details from both sides. By anticipating a client's concerns, you are making him more comfortable with your competence and sensitivity. Things like specific work schedules and firm delivery dates are of paramount importance to everyone when spending money. For instance, if I am working in a house, the customers might not want me to show up at 6:00 A.M. to do my sanding. It is better to ask them what would be a convenient time to do the on-site work. These things are also important to me in that by suggesting specific work schedules and delivery dates, there will be a self-imposed deadline which helps me to get the project done. Yes, I want the contract to work for me, but it will not even get off of the ground if it isn't signed.

While still in the proposal state, every concern should be addressed and spelled out. This includes: an accurate description of the work, material choices, finishes, delivery and installation details, the project timing and a *payment schedule.* As I mentioned earlier, a proposal is an excellent tool for designing a good contract that both parties will be happy with. The proposal stage is the time to ask for what you want in a contract. I am a firm believer in the phrase "a deal is a deal." In other words, once the contract is signed, you can't change it unless it is agreeable to both parties.

One question I can always count on in my furniture classes is "When do I get paid for my work?" This is a valid question that I don't mind answering in the least. As I said, cash flow is what makes a business operate smoothly. You cannot function as a business if you do not have regular payments from customers according to the work you are doing for them. I have found that regular (or progress) payments are also to the client's benefit.

> *You cannot function as a business if you do not have regular payments from customers according to the work you are doing for them.*

For a custom (or commission) shop such as mine, it is important to receive progress payments along the way. The terms of my contracts are pretty standard when it comes to the payment schedule. I always ask for one-third of the total contract price as a down payment at the time of signing. This one-third will cover most of the material costs so that they do not have to come out of pocket. The down payment also seals the deal, and lets me know that the client is serious. Beyond the down payment, I will usually ask for an additional one-third as a progress payment about halfway through the project. Remember, the timing is all spelled out in my proposal before we sign the contract, so there will be an agreement as to when the progress payment is dispersed. The final one-third is due upon completion of the project satisfaction of the client. This method of payment works well in my business, but it may have to be altered for other woodworking concerns. For instance, progress payments may not be in order for smaller items that take only a day to produce, but I do think that some sort of down payment should always be applied to anything that is built specifically for a client.

CHAPTER SUMMARY

- Estimating and pricing your work correctly is essential to succeeding in business. When estimating or bidding on a specific project, there are four basic areas of consideration: overhead, labor costs, materials and supplies, and profit (O, L & M). Each of these areas is as important to consider as the next when it comes to the accuracy of the bid.

- General overhead includes all of the continual costs of doing business. The costs which make up the overhead of a business include rent, furnishings, equipment payments or leases, office expenses, etc. Once these continual costs are added up and averaged on a monthly basis, they can be converted to a *per day* cost. This is done according to the specific business hours of operation.

- Labor for a project includes both physical and mental work. All of the labor invested by the owners and/or employees must be included in the bid. Any additional payroll-related expenses should be included in the bid on a per-hour basis. These payroll expenses usually amount to 50 percent of the hourly wage rate. Salary is treated in the same way as wages and should be calculated on a per-hour basis for bidding purposes.

- Materials and supplies are figured for each specific job and should always be charged at retail to the customer. Everything that goes into a project should be considered in the bid. It is wise to figure an additional 10 to 15 percent on the lumber costs for downfall and waste. Attention should be given to buying all wholesale materials (lumber) in quantity so as to realize price breaks. To save milling charges and for better quality control, lumber should be ordered rough whenever possible.

- Profit is the financial gain obtained from the use of any capital (including labor) in a transaction or series of transactions. Profit is a percentage which is added to the total of O, L & M. For the woodworking industry, 15 to 20 percent is a good average percentage to be added to a bid as profit, depending on the specific business. If a business is producing consistent profit from operation, it becomes easier to obtain credit from vendors, banks and lending institutions.

- Some projects can be approached on a time and materials (T&M) basis. This means that the customer will pay for the materials (directly or indirectly) and will also pay for the time that it takes to do a project. In cases of "unknown" cost involvement or incremental budgeting, it may be better for a contractor or craftsperson to work on a T&M basis. If possible, T&M should be approached on a "not to exceed" basis for the customer's comfort.

- A proposal is a plan that is either denied, altered or agreed upon. Unless denied, a proposal will ultimately turn into a contract. Proposals are helpful in negotiating the terms of the business at hand. A contract is a verbal or written agreement between two or more parties. Written contracts are recommended when entering any business arrangement. Both verbal and written contracts are legally binding. When using a written contract, simplicity is the key. It should include the date, all pertinent customer information, a description of the work, the terms of the agreement, and a place for the signatures.

Marketing Yourself and Your Work

In business, marketing is what makes the world go around. The word *marketing* is somewhat synonymous with selling and is the means by which products are moved from production to the consumer. Every business should have some sort of marketing plan in place before the business is opened. Good marketing consists of first planning and then executing your objective. This process can be as simple as talking to a customer on the phone or as complex as running a national advertisement on television. There are many different approaches to the marketing of products, and in this "age of information," some of those approaches seem to be ever changing. Every business is a little different from others, but the basic marketing techniques are all the same. In my mind, good marketing is "whatever works" within the confines of legality, morality and honesty.

> *Every business should have some sort of marketing plan in place before the business is opened.*

MARKETING TECHNIQUES

Depending on the category of woodworking a person is involved in, some marketing techniques will work better than others. There are many proven methods of marketing. Some of these marketing methods for the woodworking industry include:

- A good visible location (for certain businesses)
- Traditional newspaper and magazine advertising
- Radio and television advertising
- Sponsorships and donations

> *A little groundwork is always recommended so that marketing dollars are not wasted.*
>
> ———
>
> *For a woodworking business there are many low-cost marketing strategies that can be used.*

Before using any of these marketing techniques, you should have a good understanding of your particular market. Among other things, this understanding includes knowing who would be most inclined to buy your products (market base) and where these customers are physically located (demographics). A little groundwork is always recommended so that marketing dollars are not wasted. For instance, you would not want to target persons with an income of less than five thousand dollars a year if you are selling very high-end furniture.

DEVELOPING A MARKETING PLAN
Describe Your Business and the Marketplace
- What is the product or service you offer?
- Describe your target market in terms of demographics and geography.
- Analyze any market trends.
- Who is your competition and how long have they been established?
- Evaluate your competitive strengths and weaknesses.

Factors to Consider
- What are the benefits of your products?
- What are the venues for delivering your message and why?
- Long-term or short-term advertising?
- Specific advertising strategies.
- Short-term and long-term goals for specific products.
- Time frames for profitability.
- Frequent review of the plan and the necessity of staying focused.
- Updating your plan when changes occur in the market.

New business owners will always have questions like:
- When is it smart to spend money on marketing?
- How much time and money should I spend, and on what form of marketing?
- What type of marketing will yield the best return for my business?

It is up to business owners to identify their products, and then design a marketing plan specific for that business. If one-on-one assistance is needed, you can contact the local Small Business Administration (SBA). They will help you develop a good marketing program suited to your business. The SBA has toll free numbers and is also located on the Web at http://www.sba.gov.

DEVELOPING MARKETING STRATEGIES
For a woodworking business, there are many low-cost marketing strategies that can be used. For instance, by simply taking pictures of your product, you can document your company's progress and use the photographs for promotion. Some other low-cost marketing techniques, such as using the Internet, may be a matter of trial and error, but there have been many successes which show that this form of marketing can work. Traditional forms of marketing are more proven but are also more expensive. In the end, I believe that good marketing is an ongoing process and should employ a combination of techniques.

> *As a business owner you should write your own business description before attempting to develop a marketing plan.*

A Marketing Plan
A good marketing plan is an essential part of business operations. It defines how the business plans to *attract* and *retain* customers or clients. Customers are the most important part of a business—they are the means by which it will generate the income needed for operations, repay debts and produce a profit. A marketing plan should be designed to expand the customer base by identifying new clientele. The five basic requirements of a successful marketing plan are to:
- Know your product or service
- Know your customers
- Know your competitors
- Attract and retain clientele
- Identify and anticipate change

As a business owner you should write your own business description before attempting to develop a marketing plan. In doing this you will

SAMPLE PRODUCT OUTLINE

This is an example of an outline of unique features of a specific product line. Such an outline is helpful in explaining how customers will benefit and should be made prior to developing a marketing plan.

Kitchen Cabinet Line—Features

- Standard sizes for ease of installation
- European hinges which are adjustable and allow the doors to be removed easily, as for cleaning
- Full-extension drawer slides which give access to the whole drawer
- Melamine on insides of cabinets and drawers which is an easily cleaned, sanitary surface
- Choice of hardwoods for face frames, doors and drawer fronts
- Choice of finishes which make cabinets compatible with any decor
- Trained experts to take measurements and explain all cabinet options
- Installation packages available

better understand your own product. While describing your product or service, make an outline of what you feel are the unique aspects and explain how these will be important to your customers (see "Sample Product Outline" above). By emphasizing the features you feel are the best selling points, you will be better able to explain how and why they are important to your customers. In other words, the unique aspects and features of your product or service are what will be used to convince customers to buy your product instead of those of your competitors.

After the product features and potential clientele have been identified, the next factor to consider is how the message will best be delivered to the market base of customers. Some simple marketing tools include:

- Advertisements in newspapers
- Advertisements in magazines
- Display ads in phone book yellow pages
- Direct marketing via mail or phone calls
- Trade show participation
- A presence on the Internet

Marketing a new business does require a lot more energy, time and money than marketing an existing business. It takes time to get your business name out to the public. A good marketing plan for a new business is one that builds momentum and has compounding effects. The natural course of a business with marketing momentum would be a "spiraling" effect. For example, beginning with the idea, a product is created or a service is identified. The product or service is then offered to potential clients and sales are made. If customers feel your product has value, they may repeat their business and/or tell someone else about it.

A good marketing plan for a new business is one that builds momentum and has compounding effects.

Considering Advertising

Traditionally, advertising has been the backbone of a good marketing program. Advertising dollars come out of the marketing budget, and the marketing budget is derived from previous profits. For example, profit is 16 percent of the total gross revenue for a custom shop. Ten percent of that profit should be used for advertising to build future business. When business increases as a result of specific advertising, 10 percent of that profit should be used for future advertising. The profits will then have to be recovered as a result of the product advertising, which should also produce a good return on the investment. The price of the product will increase as the cost of advertising goes up. Generic products were born as a "reverse" result of this concept. Because generic products are advertised less, they are therefore more affordable.

When considering advertising of any kind, always inquire as to the circulation or exposure of the ad. In the advertising world, the words *circulation* and *exposure* refer to the number of potential customers who will see your ad. For the most part, the price of advertising in a newspaper or other print media is usually based on circulation and will go up according to the number of people it reaches. For example, a local newspaper with a circulation of 8,000 readers may charge only $100 for a one-time ad, while a major newspaper with a circulation of 200,000 may charge $500 for the same size ad. In this example, the $500 ad would reach more people per dollar spent.

> *When considering advertising of any kind, always inquire as to the circulation or exposure of the ad.*

Geographical area *demographics* are another consideration when deciding how to spend your advertising dollars. *Demography* is the study of vital statistics of any given population. In advertising, demographics are often compiled in the categories of age groups, lifestyles, areas of interest, yearly incomes and social habits. Demographic studies are for sale to the advertiser for the purpose of market planning. Armed with this information, a business that sells advertising also can target a market for advertisers. As an example, a magazine that is devoted to architecture or interior design targets a certain body of the population as potential subscribers. Consequently, this would be a good

place to advertise various types of woodworking products.

There are many levels of advertising, including local, regional, national and international. As a rule, with custom woodworking products, the further you reach out from the local level, the greater the ratio of expense to return. This is due to the actual cost of the advertising and the logistics of servicing the attracted clientele. For example, as a custom woodworker, if I attract a potential client in New York City when my shop is located in Washington, it would have cost me more (than on the local level) to place the national ad, and it will be harder to service this new client from this great distance. The cost of national advertising can sometimes be prohibitive for the custom woodworking business.

Production woodworking products are much better candidates for national and international advertising than custom woodworking products. Production items are usually packaged for shipment anyway, and they also have a broader base of customers that can afford them. Things such as craft items, furniture accessories, wooden games, kitchen accessories and some furniture items are small enough to package and ship easily. With these shipable products, the shipping and handling are added to the price of the item, and the handling charge helps pay for the advertising. These types of wood products are also good candidates for the mail order business which advertises via catalogs that are distributed per demographics.

Local and Regional Advertising

Local and regional advertising are usually more affordable to the majority of small woodworking concerns. This is especially true when the local and/or regional market base is large enough to support the business long-term. Local advertising should always be less broad in scope than regional, national and international advertising. As a result, more attention should be paid to the circulation of the advertising than to the demographics. For example, a display ad in the local phone book would be less expensive (per day) than the same size ad in a local newspaper.

> *The cost of taking pictures of your work is negligible compared to the time involved in trying to describe it to new clients with words.*

If the focus of advertising is placed at the local level, there should be an ongoing and systematic campaign. To advertise sporadically does little good in the broad-based markets. If the broad base of potential customers can see your name several times over a short time period, the return will always be better. The largest broad-base publication in the area should be where the advertising money is spent. For instance, a local newspaper may reach 75 percent of the population, but a magazine in the same area may reach only 30 percent of the same population. These two ads would probably cost the same amount of money.

Low-Cost Marketing Strategies

Regardless of the size of a business, low-cost marketing strategies are sometimes the best ones. Low-cost strategies are "long shots" in terms of the potential return versus dollars invested. Depending upon the particular marketing budget, these strategies may be all that can be employed. For the woodworking industry, some examples of good low-cost strategies would be:

- Documenting your work
- Displaying finished work
- Encouraging repeat and referral business
- Affiliation with trade associations

- Press coverage
- A Web site on the Internet

These are all strategies that will require a minimal amount of money and/or time but can produce a good yield. As a matter of fact, I am continually surprised at how many businesses do not take advantage of some of these strategies. For instance, I was recently looking for some information about a certain international tool company on the Internet and found that they did not have a presence there. Today, a lot of business will be lost to competitors without the use of this important low-cost marketing venue.

> *You can easily lose a sale if you are not prepared when a client or customer is ready to buy your product.*

Documenting Your Work

We have all heard the phrase "A picture is worth a thousand words." Nothing could be more true when it comes to woodworking. You can talk yourself blue in the face about your work, or you can just show someone pictures. Obviously, the products in the pictures don't have to be described, and there won't be any misunderstandings about the work you have done. The cost of taking pictures of your work is negligible compared to the time involved in trying to describe it to new clients with words. Also, when *good* photographs are produced for potential clients, you gain respect. Showing them photographs of your work will also keep them from asking questions like, "Well, what work have you done in the past?" While trying to determine if you are the right person for the job, potential clients must be comfortable with your competence as quickly as possible.

Documenting your finished work with photographs is of paramount importance when it comes to marketing your business for the future. True, you can send a potential client to physically view work that you have done, but how many people will take the time to do that? When your company is considered for a project (or product), it is best to try to close the deal as soon as possible. You can easily lose a sale if you are not prepared when a client is ready to buy your product. A lot of things can happen to change their mind. For example, suppose you sent prospective customers to view your work (because you did not have a picture), and on the way to the location they noticed a store that sells a product just like yours. They may stop there to get some ideas, and bingo, a better salesman makes the sale. This may sound ridiculous, but believe me: it happens every day.

Pictures of your work should always be on file for advertising and display purposes. Display ads (ads which have pictures or graphics—see "Sample Display Ad" below) usually have a

> *The more potential clients who see pictures of your work in any venue, the greater the product association with your name.*

greater impact than ads which contain "copy" (words) only. A display ad will usually cost a little more, but again, "a picture is worth a thousand words." You may seldom elect to run a picture with your ads, but if you do, be prepared by having good photographs at your disposal. The more potential clients who see pictures of your work in any venue, the greater the product association with your name.

Displaying Your Work

From a craftsman's point of view, I am a firm believer in displaying my work. Exposure is the key to any business, including mine. The more people who view my work, the more people who will

It is helpful to use pictures of your products in display ads for good product exposure.

be aware of my existence. Displaying a product in appropriate places will gain exposure on a much different level than advertising. People will notice three-dimensional examples on display more often than they would a two-dimensional ad. In my

> *Displaying a product in appropriate places will gain exposure on a much different level than advertising.*
>
> ————
>
> *Your phone number should be obvious in several places within a display.*

business, displaying my work has always accounted for a substantial percentage of my future business. Displays can be done on many levels at more than one location at the same time. On the local level, that is, in the community in which my business is located, I always have some examples of my work on display. I do this by finding other business concerns with good public foot traffic that are willing to show off my woodworking. This approach requires a little legwork and some good communication skills, but it is well worth the effort. Some good locations for displaying finished work include:

- Restaurants
- Banks
- Hotel lobbies
- Movie theaters
- Airports

Along with the work that is being displayed, some sort of business brochure or business card should be available. Your phone number should be obvious in several places within the display. I always include a craftsman's profile (expanded resume) within my display so interested parties can read about my completed major projects,

qualifications, education, etc. People enjoy reading about artists and craftspeople, and sometimes this alone will sell you as a person who does good work.

Another way of displaying completed projects is by the use of good photographs. It is sometimes hard to find businesses with enough floor space to display your physical work. A good alternative to this is to find a business with a plain wall that you can use. I have always taken this added approach in my career, and it has always given me great results. If a business owner is reluctant to let you display your photographs, offer to pay rent for the space. A fair price for this would be thirty to fifty dollars a month depending on the size of the wall. Think about it: a written ad in a major newspaper would cost you ten times that much for just one day. By renting a wall you can have the lasting benefits of term (extended period of time) advertising, displaying your work, and having brochures available for anyone who is interested.

> *If a product is located in high traffic areas, ongoing exposure is realized.*

Using Commercial Woodwork as Advertising

For my type of a woodworking business (custom), it is smart to be involved in a certain percentage of what I call "commercial" work. Commercial work is work which is done for business concerns located in a public place. If a product is located in high traffic areas, ongoing exposure is realized. Restaurants, banks, offices and hotels are all good examples of businesses that have a lot of traffic. If work is done for other business concerns, that's an automatic endorsement that I don't have to pay for. I am actually getting paid to have my work on "display" at these establishments. While commercial work is more nerve-racking by the nature of the pace, it is also more beneficial in terms of the exposure. I have always tried to design my workload to be about 50 percent commercial work and 50 percent private work at any given time. My point of view here is that the commercial work will bring me the private work. The more people can view my work in professional establishments that they frequent, the more a connection will be made with my work. With this approach I have also realized new clientele other than the local population (tourists), who will in turn spread the word even further.

Getting Repeat Business and Referrals

Of all the means by which new business is obtained, repeat and referral business is the best type. Repeat business means that your customer or client was happy enough with your product to come back and buy again. I count on this happening every time I build something for a new customer. This does not happen naturally, but is in fact another form of good marketing. How you treat your customers each time you do work for them will determine if they come back or not. If the business experience was good and the customers are happy with the work you did for them, they will always keep you in mind for future projects. Conversely, if the experience was unpleasant, or the customers did not like your product, they will be unhappy and can do your business harm. For example, if clients are unhappy with you or your work, they will not consider your product in the future and, what is worse, they will tell others of their bad experience. I have a saying posted in my shop which reads, *"If you are happy with me and my work, tell your friends. If you are unhappy with me or my work, please tell me."* A sign like this posted in your office will let your customers know you are anxious to do your best work for them.

In the woodworking industry, referral business is all business that is obtained by someone referring you, your work or your business to someone new. What better form of new business could there be? A referral customer will be someone who believes in you before you even talk to them. I would say that one-third of my new business is a result of referrals. Benefiting from referral business can result from something as simple as someone dropping your name (in a good way), to compliments from an overzealous client "raving" about the furniture item that you made for him. Whatever the case may be, new customers come to see you because they have heard something good. More will be said about repeat and referral business in chapter eight, "Attitude and Working With People."

Joining Trade Associations and Organizations

Woodworking trade associations and organizations are a wonderful low-cost source of obtaining current trade information and advertising venues, and a way to meet like-minded people. There are local, regional, national and international associations and organizations. These will usually offer:

- Statistical information
- Business information
- Marketing information
- Books and reports (publications)
- Consulting services
- Mailing lists and directories
- Industry standards
- Current news
- Resources
- Industry calendars (conventions and conferences)

A lot of this information is offered free, especially from the nonprofit organizations. Other organizations and associations offer their services for a low membership fee and periodic dues. Those involved with woodwork marketing should at least make themselves aware of as many of these organizations as possible and join the ones which pertain directly to their business (see list of Trade Associations and Organizations). Trade associations and organizations are made up of committed administrators, industry suppliers, industry experts and competitors sharing information. Most of the bigger trade associations and organizations can be contacted by phone, via the mail, and will also have a Web site with E-mail capability.

Getting Press Coverage

There is no form of advertising as good as free, positive press coverage. This is not as difficult to obtain as one might think. There are literally thousands of newspapers, magazines, and television and radio stations in existence. Each one of these entities employs writers who are hungry for a story. There is always someone willing to write about your craftsmanship or your special product. A feature article has far greater impact on the public than advertising does. If you can obtain this type of press coverage, the benefits will be far-reaching. A positive article or story is an en-

TRADE ASSOCIATIONS AND ORGANIZATIONS

Woodworking trade associations and organizations are wonderful low-cost sources of obtaining current trade information and advertising venues, and are a way to meet like-minded people.

International Wood Products Association (IHPA)
4214 King St. W.
Alexandria, VA 22302
Phone: (703) 820-6696
Fax: (703) 820-8550
Web site: http://www.transport.com/~leje/ihpa.html

Western Wood Products Association (WWPA)
522 S.W. Fifth Ave., Suite 500
Portland, OR 97204-2122
Phone: (503) 224-3930
Fax: (503) 224-3934
Web site: http://www.wwpa.org/

Aktrin Furniture Information Center
P.O. Box 898
High Point, NC 27261
Phone: (336) 841-8535
Fax: (336) 841-5435
Canadian office:
151 Randall St.
Oakville, ON L6J 1P5 Canada
Phone: (905) 845-3474
Fax: (905) 845-7459
Web site: http://www.aktrin.com/

Architectural Woodwork Institute
1952 Isaac Newton Square W.
Reston, VA 20190
Phone: (703) 733-0600
Fax: (703) 733-0584
Web site: http://www.awinet.org/

> *There is no form of advertising as good as free, positive press coverage.*

dorsement by the publisher that can be used for future marketing strategies. For example, an article in a local newspaper can be framed and posted in a wall display. Building a *mystique* around a business is part of good marketing.

There are several ways to go about obtaining free press coverage. If your business is new, most local newspapers will publish a story in their business section. This is a service of the paper to its readers and is also free to the businessperson. Beyond the new business article, each time you place an ad in a new or different publication you should contact the editor of that publication. Armed with a current portfolio (pictures of your product) and the fact that you just placed an ad, you can suggest the possibility of an article or story about your business. Get editors interested in what you do for a living and the fact that you are also a businessperson in their city, state or country.

Marketing on the Internet

One of my favorite woodworking class and seminar topics is "Woodworking on the Internet." In these classes I take a "foundational" approach to the Internet in general and how it applies to woodworking. One of the first things I discuss is the fact that the Internet as a marketing tool appears to be here to stay. According to everything I know and am learning about the subject, however, the Internet is still in its infancy. This means that there are still a lot of doors to be opened and the "sky is the limit." That is exciting when you think about the expense of traditional methods of marketing and the possibilities of this newest vehicle.

Believe me when I say you don't have to be a brain surgeon to make the Internet work for you. I'm not a brain surgeon, and it works for me. Presently, Internet-generated sales represent about 15 percent of my total gross sales. That is astounding to me considering how very little I have invested into the Internet. This business was generated via my Web page. Since it was designed and built, this page has cost me about $25 a month to be hosted by a server (on-line service). You can't even get a display ad in a local phone book for that cost. The page design itself cost about $175 which included scanning (converting photographs into computer images) pictures of my work.

To take advantage of the Internet as a marketing tool, of course, you need access to a computer. This doesn't mean you have to *own* a computer, but only have access to one. When getting started with this marketing concept, you can use a library computer. Most local libraries have computers that can be accessed with your library card. This is a great way to experiment with the technology, and it won't cost you anything. Most schools (elementary through college) also have computers with on-line (connected to the Internet) capabilities which can be accessed by the student body and sometimes the parents of the students. Private computer labs, located in most major cities, will rent computer time at a reasonable cost. I first learned about the Internet in a coffee shop which also sold computer time. Also, you may have friends and relatives with computers who will let you "explore" with their equipment until you decide to get your own. These are all great ways to become familiar with what the Internet has to offer you in the way of marketing your product.

When getting started with the Internet, it is a

good idea to "search" for Web pages of other woodworking companies to see how they are set up. I have set up my Web site to be partly information for other woodworkers or anyone who is interested in my craft for any reason. On my pages I post things such as descriptions of my work (with pictures), woodworking articles I have written, and "hyper links" (an easy means of accessing other Web pages) to other woodworking sites. Among other things, this information will hold the interest of someone who is visiting my site. If they like what they see, they may be more inclined to inquire about the work itself or mention it to someone else who may need my services. Somewhere in the middle of my site, I have included a profile of myself as a craftsman and a resume of my work through the years. This information is helpful when someone is looking for a craftsman with abilities like mine.

I am constantly updating my site, which also contains my national seminar schedule for the coming season. Among other reasons, I update because some people may wish to visit my site more than once. If they just see the same information over and over, they might be less inclinned to check back again. Another reason for updating is to post new pictures of my work. This shows my versatility and the fact that my business is successful. There are tremendous psychological benefits when a potential client sees ongoing progress in a craftsman's career.

Along with a Web site you will be given an E-mail (electronic mail) address. This address is your link to all who view your Web site, and is how you will communicate (at least at first) with anyone who is interested in your work. Eventually, if there is more than general interest, communication may also be by phone, fax or mail. In the old days (three or four years ago), when first corresponding with a new client on the other side of the country, it was very expensive and time-consuming. At that time it was necessary to send pictures of my work through the mail and then follow up with a phone call to the potential client, hoping that he would still be interested. After all was said and done it, was sometimes as long as a month from the time the process began, and I could only hope that my pictures would be returned in good shape. Now, since I have a Web site, I can quite simply give my Universal Resource Locator (URL) or Web address to inquiring clients, and ask them to view my work there. Believe it or not, 90 percent of the time if they don't have a computer of their own, they will find one and look me up. Must be the challenge!

USING YOUR COMPUTER

Owning or having access to a computer can be a wonderful asset to your business. I feel that a computer can be as valuable to a woodworking business as the table saw. A computer not only provides Internet access, it's also a tool for conducting written correspondence, developing marketing ideas, producing shop drawings and communicating electronically. In this age of information and fast-paced communications, the computer is rapidly becoming an essential part of doing business.

Any business requires communication. This

communication should always be professional or it will not be taken seriously. *Word processing programs* are easily acquired and reasonably priced. These programs are "user friendly" (easy to use) and will make your correspondence look very professional. Company letterhead can be updated easily, and documents can be stored for future reference or editing. If the computer is outfitted with fax capabilities, you can send a letter without ever having to print it out.

Desktop publishing programs will allow the user to create a multitude of marketing products. These programs are also reasonably priced and easy to use. Multiuse programs can create business forms, brochures, business cards, Web pages and many other helpful marketing tools. These items can also be stored in your computer for future updating or reference.

Computer Assisted Design (CAD) programs are somewhat more complex, but have become the industry standard for interior and exterior architectural drawings. These programs are a little more expensive than word processing and desktop publishing programs, but are well worth the price. Once learned, they can make short work of perspective drawings, three-dimensional drawings, conceptual drawings, exploded drawings, and just about anything else you would care to draw.

CHAPTER SUMMARY

- The word *marketing* is somewhat synonymous with *selling*. Every business should have a good marketing plan. Marketing involves first planning and then executing your objective. There are many proven methods of marketing yourself and your business. There are also many low-cost marketing strategies that may result in a high percentage of return.
- A marketing plan defines how you plan to attract and retain customers or clients. A sales plan defines how you will generate the income needed for operations, to repay debts and produce a profit. A marketing plan should also consider expansion of the customer base by identifying new clientele and by identifying and anticipating changes in the market or business. A good marketing plan should be one that builds momentum and has compounding effects.
- Advertising is the backbone of a good marketing program. The price of products will increase as advertising costs go up. Circulation or exposure is the most important thing to consider when advertising is purchased. There are many levels of advertising which include local, regional, national and international. Production woodworking items are better candidates for national and international advertising than custom woodworking products. Local and regional advertising is usually more affordable to small woodworking concerns.
- Documenting your woodwork with photographs is important to marketing your product. The cost of taking a picture is negligible compared to the time involved in trying to prove yourself with words. Photographs of your work can also be used for advertising and displays. The more pictures you have, the better exposure you can achieve.
- Low-cost marketing strategies are those that require a minimal investment of money and/or time but produce a good yield. Some low-cost marketing strategies for woodwork include: displaying finished work, encouraging repeat and referral business, affiliations with trade associations, press coverage and a Web site.
- Good exposure is gained by displaying finished woodwork. Good business locations for displaying your finished work include

restaurants, banks, hotel lobbies, movie theaters and airports. When work is displayed it is important to have some printed information that includes your phone number which interested parties can take home with them. Woodworking can also be displayed with photographs on walls in businesses or other public locations.

- Involvement with commercial woodwork will also afford good exposure. Products purchased and used by other businesses are in effect an endorsement by the business. Commercial concerns such as restaurants, banks, offices and hotels generate a lot of viewers for your work. For custom woodworking shops, a good balance of clientele would be 50 percent commercial and 50 percent private. Commercial exposure will help bring in new private projects and can also have a compounding effect on your commercial business.

- Repeat and referral business is the best type of new business. Repeat and referral business is generated by customers who are happy with your work. How you treat your customers is directly correlated to repeat and referral business. Unhappy customers can have a negative effect on future business.

- Woodworking trade associations and organizations are a low-cost source of marketing ideas and contacts. There are local, regional, national and international woodworking associations and organizations which offer statistical business information, consulting services, directories, resources and industry convention and conference calendars.

- Positive press coverage is a good form of free advertising. An article written about your work has far greater marketing impact than paid advertising. A positive article or story is an endorsement that can be used for future

marketing strategies. Most local newspapers will publish a story about a new business in their business section. Try to generate an article about your work each time you place an ad somewhere new.

- The Internet is a relatively new and low-cost marketplace that appears to be here to stay. A Web site on the Internet is relatively inexpensive and is a good presence for your business. Before designing a Web page, search for pages of other woodworking companies to see how they market themselves. Web pages should be informational, including pictures and a personal or business profile. Web sites should be periodically updated. An E-mail address is a benefit of having a Web site and allows you to communicate with potential customers.

- A computer can be an asset to your business. It can be used for conducting written correspondence, developing marketing ideas, producing drawings and communicating on-line. For woodwork, inexpensive software is available for desktop publishing, Web page design, computer-assisted drawing and word processing applications.

6

Shop Efficiency and Saving Money on Operations

THE SHOP LAYOUT

The physical layout of a woodworking shop is very important when it comes to efficiency. The number of steps required to accomplish a goal can be minimized with the proper layout. Shop efficiency will quickly translate into money saved on a daily basis by:

- Reducing man hours in the shop
- Increasing the productivity of the shop
- Reducing material waste
- Increasing usable floor space
- Realizing the best use of equipment
- Encouraging good organizational practices

These savings are especially apparent when the business maintains employees, and an efficient layout has the added benefit of improving shop safety. The "operations" department is the heart of any business. Without operations, there would be no need for sales, accounting, shipping or any of the other departments that make up a business. For a woodworking business the proper placement of stationary power tools and workbenches and good general organization practices are the keys to efficient operations. This chapter will consider the different aspects of typical woodworking operations and how they can be made cost-efficient.

I have designed a shop layout which can be very efficient for most woodworking situations (see "Basic Shop Layout," p. 62). Based on a space 35' × 26', this equipment layout would be appropriate for most small shops, but the propor-

tions can always be expanded if necessary. This particular shop size was selected as a minimum requirement to comfortably accommodate the tools shown. This layout can also be found in my book *Tune Up Your Tools* (Betterway Books), which elaborates upon the placement and maintenance of each individual piece of equipment. Depending on the size of the work space and the type of woodworking business, you may need to make alterations in my general shop plan, but at least I will have started you thinking.

> *For a woodworking business the proper placement of stationary power tools and workbenches and good general organization practices are the keys to efficient operations.*

My layout is based on what I call the "golden triangle" of woodworking (see "Golden Triangle Layout," p. 63). The golden triangle is usually associated with cooking and the kitchen, but I have always maintained that woodworking is similar to cooking, in that several things must be "simmering" at once to get the projects finished on time. For both woodworking and cooking, if your work stations are not set up to be efficient you will be "tripping over your own feet." The golden triangle of woodworking includes three basic

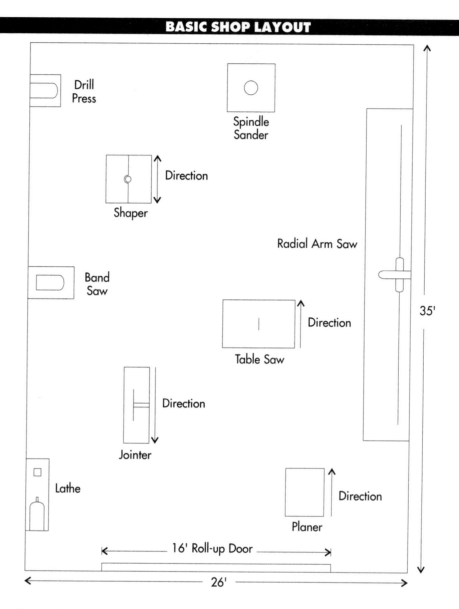

The minimum size for a small custom or production shop should be about 26' × 35'. There should be at least one wide receiving and/or shipping door at one end of the building. Note the direction of feed on the linear feed machinery.

pieces of equipment: the table saw, the jointer and the radial arm (or crosscut) saw. These three tools should be placed close to each other in order to save steps. As I explain my layout, I will also give some recommendations on equipment sizes for an average woodworking shop.

The Golden Triangle

The table saw is undoubtedly the most important tool in the shop, and should be placed between the radial arm saw and jointer. The table saw must also be situated in a way to provide plenty of room on all sides of the blade for ripping and crosscutting (at least enough for a piece of plywood). My standard layout shows the table saw close to the center of the shop. This is fine when there is adequate space, but may not work if the shop is smaller than my layout shows. One thing that can be done when space is an issue is to place the "feed end" of the saw close to a door that can be opened when ripping long pieces (see "Golden Triangle in a Confined Space,"

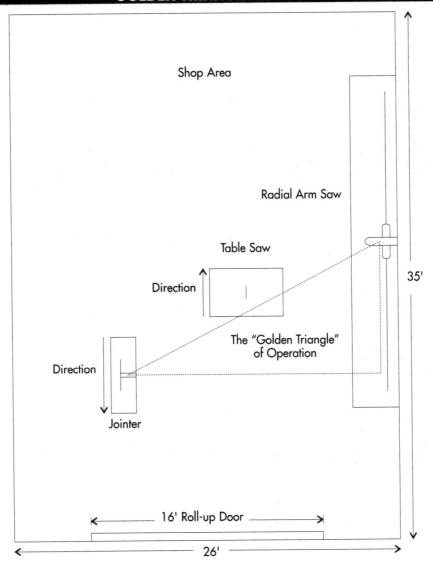

Shop Area

Radial Arm Saw

Table Saw

35'

Direction

The "Golden Triangle" of Operation

Direction

Jointer

16' Roll-up Door

26'

The "golden triangle" of operation includes the table saw, radial arm saw and jointer. These pieces of equipment should be close to each other in order to save steps.

p. 64). For example, occasionally I do work on wooden boats which requires ripping 26'-long pieces of material. My shop is about 50' long, so even if I had the center of the blade in the middle of the room, I would not have enough room with the doors closed to do this job. Therefore, in my shop I have placed the saw at one-third of the depth and close to the roll-up door that I use for receiving materials. This orientation works well during normal operations, but if necessary I can open the door for added distance behind the blade. The industry standard for table saws in most furniture and cabinet shops is the stationary 10″ saw (10″ refers to the diameter of the blade). The stationary base affords stability, and the 10″-diameter blade will comfortably cut material that is 3″ thick.

It's a real toss-up whether the radial arm saw or the jointer is more important. I consider them both indispensable, but if I had to choose, I would lean towards the jointer. Most of the functions of the radial arm saw could be done on the table saw,

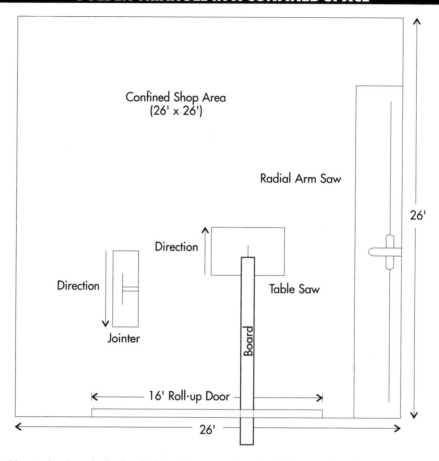

When space is a problem in the shop, the feed end of the table saw can be placed close to a door that can be opened to provide additional length for the cut.

although this would decrease shop efficiency due to the setup time involved. The jointer is quite specific and can make you money (and save material) by allowing you to purchase material that is not dimensioned (straight-lined on one edge, and then ripped to width). In any event, if you have a jointer it should be placed as close to the table saw as possible without affecting the saw's operation. The ideal location would be to place the jointer near the left feed end of the saw. When placed this way, the direction of feed for the jointer should be opposite the direction of feed for the table saw. With this saw/jointer orientation, steps are saved when doing production jointing and ripping operations for extended periods of time. One need only turn and take a few steps while moving between these two pieces of equipment. If you are buying a

jointer, I recommend an 8″ (width of the blade) rather than a 6″ one, because the 8″ jointer comes with a minimum 5′-long bed and increases the maximum width of cut by 2″. If a 6″ jointer is more affordable, then try to find one with a long bed (5′ long).

The third piece of equipment within the golden triangle would be the radial arm saw. A miter (or chop) saw is also nice to have, but it doesn't replace the radial saw when it comes to width of cut. Even compound, sliding miter saws will only cut material that is 12″ wide. The radial saw is used for many purposes including crosscutting, mitering and overhead dadoing, as well as some exotic operations. It too should be placed close to the table saw, preferably on the side opposite to the jointer. It should also be oriented against the longest wall in the shop, so this fact might affect the orientation of all three tools. The reasoning here is the same as with the relationship of the jointer to the table saw. Steps can be saved while working between the radial and table saws. The radial saw should be fixed to a flat and level long bench, which in essence becomes part of the tool. A 12″ (diameter of the blade) radial saw with an 18″-24″ throw (distance that the saw can be pulled) is my recommendation here.

THE OTHER STATIONARY POWER TOOLS IN THE SHOP

Depending on the product, all the other power tools in the shop can be as important to a particular operator as the tools within the golden triangle. For the most part, these other tools can be placed against the remaining walls in the shop and possibly on wheels. The following tools are all good candidates for perimeter wall placement: the bandsaw (12″-14″ throat or distance between the blade and body of the saw); the drill press (12″ throat or distance between the bit and the support post); and the lathe (36″ between centers and 12″ diameter capacity between the centers and the bed). If a shaper (¾″ spindle diameter) is used, this tool can be placed somewhat close to a wall. Distance in front and behind the shaper cutter in line with the fence will be necessary according to typical operations. Shapers do require some room in back of the cutter when the fence is removed for collar-shaping operations. If you use a "fixed" position surface planer (12″ minimum blade width), this tool can be stationed close to an exterior door if long boards are to be surfaced.

Whenever possible, stationary compressors and large vacuum systems should be mounted somewhere outside the work space. Both of these tools function as the heart of their perspective "systems" and do not need to be located within valuable work space. There is also a noise

factor associated with both of these machines that can become a nuisance when trying to concentrate. I recommend that noise-insulated enclosures of some sort be made on the exterior of the shop building. Depending on whether or not the building has a raised foundation, the appropriate system can be run either under the floor or overhead. Concerning the exhaust system, it is always better if it can be run under the floor, especially if the ceiling is only 8′ high. The system can then be run directly to the base of each stationary machine and gravity will help exhaust the waste. Machines with higher cubic feet per minute (CFM) are usually required when an overhead system is employed.

In larger shops, for efficiency's sake, it is a good idea to use separate "work stations" for different types of operations.

Workbenches and Handheld Power Tools

The proper placement of workbenches is always a matter of opinion. I favor at least one "island" type of bench that can be accessed from all four sides. If room in the shop does not allow such a bench, a "peninsula" bench (which is accessed from three sides) can be designed to attach to a wall (see "Peninsula Work Bench," p. 67). Also keep in mind that if a long bench is built for the radial arm saw, it can also double as a workbench at times. In any event, workbenches should be made as strong as possible (2×4 construction or better), and should also incorporate at least one shelf below the work surface. This construction also increases efficiency. The shelf not only strengthens the bench so that the benchtop will not warp or sag, but it also provides storage for handheld power tools, sandpaper, etc., saving steps at the work station.

In larger shops, for efficiency's sake, it is a good idea to use separate "work stations" for different types of operations . For instance, one station could be used just for sanding operations in production shops. This station, comprised of a bench and all the appropriate sanding tools, should be situated close to an exterior exhaust fan. The exhaust fan would then exhaust all of the dust not captured by dust collectors. By having the sanding operations separated from the area in which things are built, a certain amount of efficiency will be gained by not confusing the two operations. If all the major shop functions can be categorized and separated, efficiency will be realized.

> *It is best to maintain tools and equipment on a "preventive" basis before or after business hours.*
>
> ---
>
> *A maintenance schedule for every power tool in the shop should be kept in a convenient place.*

TOOL MAINTENANCE

As the author of *Tune Up Your Tools*, I can't let this chapter go by without talking about the importance of ongoing tool maintenance. Continual maintenance of equipment is necessary for several reasons. Accuracy and safety are the most important of these reasons, but production efficiency runs a close third. It is very costly when tools are constantly breaking down while work is "in progress." Production stops, and all involved are idle until the problems are resolved. It is best to maintain tools and equipment on a "preventive" basis before or after business hours. By attacking maintenance in this way, it does not

> *It is far better to enter into business with sufficient equipment that is affordable than to go into burdensome debt before even getting started.*

interfere with production and can be given the time it deserves.

A maintenance schedule for every power tool in the shop should be kept in a convenient place. If this is done, everyone concerned with the equipment can access the information. Among other things, these maintenance schedules should list all the important parts to be maintained of the specific tool, and the dates on which they where last serviced. These schedules then become a matter of record, and are available to all involved with the equipment. These records not only help maintain tool longevity and accuracy, but they are also impressive to a prospective buyer if the equipment becomes for sale when upgrading or for any other reason (see "Machinery Maintenance Schedule," p. 68).

UPGRADING AND SHOPPING FOR EQUIPMENT

There is no doubt that if money were "no object" a good craftsperson would have the best equipment available. Most of the time this isn't the case, especially when a person is first starting out in business. It is far better to enter into business with sufficient equipment that is affordable than to go into burdensome debt before even getting started. In other words, buy what is needed (or a little better), and as money allows, upgrade accordingly. Upgrading equipment along the way as it can be afforded (and justified) is a wonderful option. By taking this "upgrade" approach with

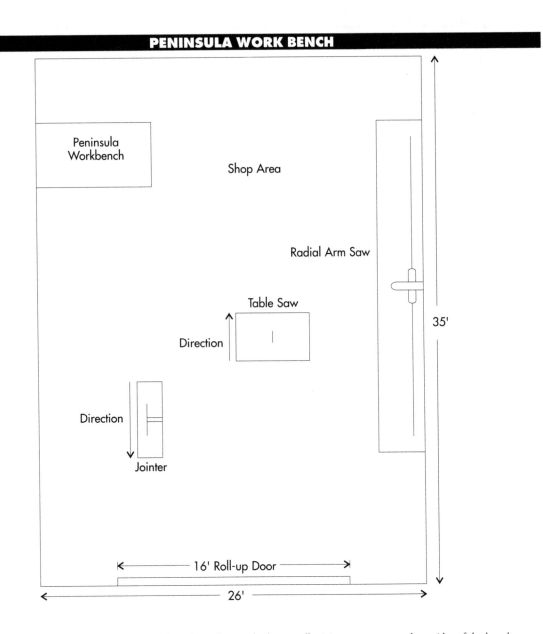

Peninsula
Workbench

Shop Area

Radial Arm Saw

Table Saw

Direction

35'

Direction

Jointer

16' Roll-up Door

26'

When shop space is a problem, a peninsula work bench can be attached to a wall, giving you access to three sides of the bench.

equipment, much benefit is realized. For one thing you can pay for these upgrades "out of pocket" as you go. A more important benefit is that you can keep current with new innovations that apply to your particular business. I always have one eye open to what equipment is available and at what price. I always keep abreast of current market prices, new equipment models (which may render previous models less useful) and what is going on in the "used" markets.

It is always fun to buy something brand new, but buying good used equipment will save money. Any depreciation (from new to used) that occurs has already been absorbed by the person who bought the tool when it was new. Of course, used equipment must be scrutinized before you buy it. Among other things, I always take a look at the reason someone is selling the equipment before I consider buying it. Is he going out of business? Did he inherit the tool? Is he upgrading

MACHINERY MAINTENANCE SCHEDULE

TOOL/MACHINE:

MANUFACTURER:

SERIAL NUMBER:

DATE OF PURCHASE:

PARTS TO BE ALIGNED:

PARTS TO BE OILED:

PARTS TO BE WAXED:

DATE	HOURS OF OPERATION	MAINTENANCE NOTES

For longevity and accuracy's sake it is always a good idea to keep a maintenance schedule like this one for every power tool in the shop. Note that the top of the sheet contains all the information needed to maintain the tool properly.

his equipment? Or is it just a piece of junk? A good understanding of the particular piece of equipment to be purchased is paramount when buying used tools.

On the other end of the spectrum, when you are selling your used equipment for upgrade purposes, it is good to be armed with certain information. This is where your maintenance schedules are very important. It is quite impressive to a prospective buyer when such a document is produced. I have never had a problem getting my asking price once a person realizes how well my tools have been maintained. Usually I am able to sell a piece of equipment for what I paid for it, and sometimes I even make money on the deal. It all depends on how I bought the tool, but that is part of good shopping. So with this approach I can buy a good used tool, use it for a period of time and then sell it without it costing me anything.

MATERIAL STORAGE

Material storage is a big concern for any type of woodworking operation. Regardless of how we pay for our square footage (rent, lease, own), shop floor space is a commodity. This fact is part of the "balancing act" which I referred to in chapter four when talking about quantity buying. It would be pointless to buy a thousand feet of lumber at a good price for further use, and then spend a dollar a square foot to store it for six months. Obviously, the money saved on the quantity buying would be outweighed by the cost of storing the material.

Some solutions do exist for cost-effective material storage. If one had the privilege of designing the ideal building to work in, I would suggest that it be built on a raised perimeter foundation. Long-term lumber storage could then be incorporated underneath the actual work space and out of the way. Of course, we do not all have this

> *When looking for shop space to buy or rent, it is wise to try to find a space with an existing loft that can be used for material and/or finished-product storage.*

privilege and have to work within our means. Some more realistic material storage solutions for existing shops include: overhead or loft storage, horizontal wall rack storage, vertical wall rack storage, exterior lean-to space and satellite (or separate building) storage space.

Overhead or loft storage is only possible when there is sufficient height in the building. When looking for shop space to buy or rent, it is wise to try to find a space with an existing loft that can be used for material and/or finished-product storage. If a building is tall enough to accommodate a loft and one does not exist, at least there is potential for building one. A loft is a wonderful solution to the storage problem because the lumber is stored nearby but does not affect the actual work space below. The only drawback to loft storage is the fact that items being stored have to be carried up and down. When negotiating to lease a space that is tall enough but does not have a loft, find out if the landlord will participate in building one.

If you can't find a building tall enough for a loft, look for a space with high ceilings (taller than 8'). High ceilings are always a good idea in a shop anyway, but they are especially nice when trying to solve a material storage problem. Horizontal racks can then be designed high on the perimeter walls and used to store a great deal of lumber. A quantity of material can be taken down when needed for a project and kept close by until actually used. The only drawback of wall racks is the fact that you can't

Finished products should be shipped or delivered immediately after they are completed.

"flip through" the stack as easily as you can with other storage solutions.

Vertical wall racks (or partitions) can also work well for storing lumber. Not as much material can be stored this way compared to the horizontal method, but it does get the wood off the floor. This method of storage will also require a high ceiling or wall if the material is over eight feet long. Partitions are easy to build and keep the materials segregated. It is also much easier to look through the material when vertical as opposed to horizontal racks are used. One drawback to this method is that if the material is kept in this vertical position for too long, it may tend to bow or warp. Lumber is always better stored flat in a dry atmosphere, and if lumber is going to be stored for any length of time, it is best stored flat and with stickers (perpendicular wooden divisions) between the layers.

Lean-to material storage outside a building is always a good option when extra space is needed. A lean-to is quite simply a roof which is attached to an existing exterior wall and is supported with either posts or another wall. The lean-to will keep the material out of the main work space and also keep it at ground level. Unlike loft or horizontal rack storage, there are no ladders or stairs to climb. If you can't find a space that has a loft or excessive ceiling height, a lean-to is the next best option. Even if the building you are looking at doesn't have an existing lean-to, check to see if there is room to build one. Keep in mind that if you are seeking to rent or lease the space, you will have to obtain permission from the owner to erect

the lean-to, and that would best be done before signing the papers.

The satellite (or separate) building method of storage may or may not be a good idea. It depends on the size of the business and how fast it will use large quantities of material. If your business is a small one-person shop, it may not pay to invest in separate storage space. Of course, the separate storage space may be something you already have control of, such as a garage or shed on another piece of property. The bottom line here is that the separate storage should be of minimal cost in order to justify buying more wood than you need for current projects. The satellite storage space should also be close to your actual work space, or transportation logistics can become a significant cost factor.

FINISHED PRODUCT STORAGE

For the most part, finished products should be shipped or delivered immediately after they are completed. This has more to do with damage liability than not wanting to store the items. The longer products sit around in the shop after they are completed, the more likelihood that they are going to get damaged. Once finished products are delivered to the client and accepted, they are no longer your responsibility. In other words, your part of the contract is completed when the product is delivered. Also, if you remember the section about contracts in chapter four, final payment will be due upon completion of the project. This in itself should be a good incentive for delivering the finished product promptly.

Sometimes, though, it is necessary to store finished work. There are many reasons that finished products cannot be delivered after completion:

- A customer is not ready for delivery at the job site.
- The item must be crated or packaged prior to shipping.

- The product was finished before schedule.
- The product is part of a total project that is not yet completed.

Regarding this last point, for example, on some of my bigger projects there may be twenty sections to the total project, and installation can't begin until all the sections have been completed. Consequently, it is necessary to temporarily store the finished sections. These finished items are stored somewhere other than the work space so they will not be in harm's way, but more importantly so they will not interfere with the ongoing efficiency of the shop.

As with material storage, product storage does cost money. This is especially true when the products are large. Unlike material storage, furniture or cabinet shop finished products normally will require floor space. This fact will limit the type of storage facility to one that has floor space. In other words, you can't easily store a cabinet on a overhead shelf or vertical rack. The loft space is a good option, but this requires that the item be taken up the stairs or ladder, and then brought back down again for delivery. Obviously, the lean-to or satellite (interim) spaces are the best bet. Again, if a satellite space is used, it can be located anywhere, including in a garage. The key here is to spend as little on the *safe*, temporary storage as possible, and it should require a minimum of effort and time to access when moving the products.

PRODUCTION FLOW

The term "production flow" refers to the way materials are received, processed and then distributed. A good production flow would be one that receives the materials at one end of the building, processes the materials in the main part (or center), and then ships the finished products from the opposite end of the building (see "Production Workflow," p. 72). With this kind of flow, there is no convergence of materials and finished products at one end of the building. As with the equipment orientation, trimming "steps" from the actual production process will save time and, of course, money. Again, this is especially true when more than one person is involved in the production process.

The first part of the production flow is receiving and storing materials. There should be a receiving door at one end of the shop that is large enough to accommodate the largest item that will be received. This is another reason to consider a building with a raised perimeter foundation. If the floor level of the shop is at the same height as the bed of the trucks, there will be less lifting involved in unloading materials. More important than having a raised loading dock, however, is having the receiving end of the shop closest to where the materials will be stored.

The next part or "body" of the production flow is the millwork and assembly. This process is also known in our industry as "fabrication" and should be done in a systematic and concise manner with as few steps as possible. During fabrication and finishing, the workers should be positioned at stations that are equipped with all the tools necessary for their particular job. In other words, it is false economy when two stations are constantly trying to use the same tools at the same time. The production line should be a natural flow within itself so as to save precious steps.

The final part of the production flow is product packaging and distribution. When finished products need to be packaged prior to delivery, it adds a step that will become part of the total production flow. Depending on the size of the operation, this packaging aspect could be a process in itself (and require its own space), but let's assume that your business is not that big yet. In either case, packaging will probably require a station of its own within the total production flow.

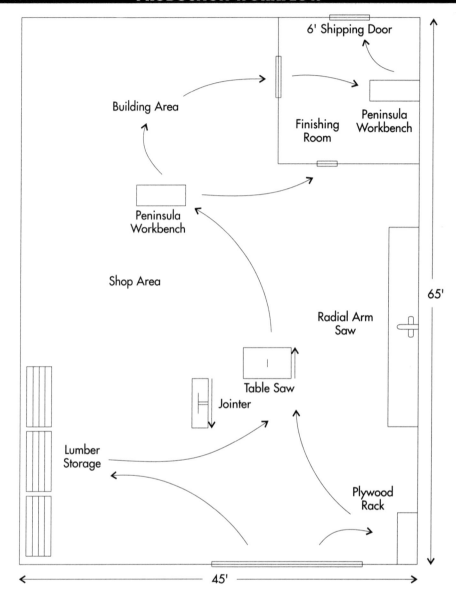

A good production flow for a woodworking business would be one that receives and stores materials at one end of the building, produces a product in the main part, and then ships the finished products from the opposite end of the building.

That station should obviously be at the end of the building closest to the shipping area. Sometimes, in small operations, there is just one door for both shipping and receiving. In that case, it may be impossible to do the packaging close to the door without affecting operations.

The actual shipping or delivery aspect of the business can be as simple as loading one cabinet a month onto a truck, or as complex as loading ten trucks a day. Each shop situation is different,

and the facility should be designed accordingly. If shipping is a major part of the business, then it should be efficient within itself. Again, the shipping and receiving areas should be at opposite ends of the building and away from the area in which products are fabricated and finished.

EFFICIENT MATERIAL USE

After bidding a few jobs you'll find that the material often represents one-third of the total bid, and the problem is getting worse. Going back to my thoughts in chapter four about materials as a commodity, it seems the price always goes up, never down. With this in mind, every cut will count and should be well thought out. I have known companies that were run well in all other areas except material use and have gone out of business as a result of inefficiency in that area. An inexperienced worker who is not properly trained in material use can do a lot of damage to a company. If you are paying an employee $7.50 an hour to cut parts for your operation and he is wasting 50 percent of your material, it may be better to close the doors and go fishing. Constant attention must be paid to efficient material use in any woodworking operation!

When first bidding a job, a good estimator will consider the best use of the materials. If this plan is not conveyed to the actual operator, profit may go out the window. It is far better to spend a little time with an operator explaining how the job was figured, than to spend time "chewing him out" because he wasted material. This is especially true when multiples of the same job are being cut. As an example, if there are twenty typical cabinets to be cut all at the same time and a fundamental error is made in planning how the parts will be cut, the error will be multiplied by twenty. Good material usage is common sense to most people who have to pay the bills, but unless this common sense is explained to operators, they may have no other way of knowing.

In the woodworking industry, solid material (lumber) is more difficult to estimate than panels (plywood, etc.). With panels there is very little waste due to defects such as knots and splits. Un-

less we handpick our lumber, however, solid stock can be a big variable in terms of usage. When ordering lumber, it is often necessary to specify not only the grade of material but also some specific lengths and widths. In other words, if a cutting list requires that a multitude of 8″ parts be cut, then it would be pointless to order material that is only available in 6″ widths. This may sound silly, but I have known of many situations where the person responsible for ordering neglected to mention some very pertinent facts, and then was unpleasantly surprised upon delivery of the material. In such a case, progress is delayed while waiting for the proper materials to arrive.

Although panel products have little waste due to defects, a cutting list must always be thoroughly thought out. Plywood is not cheap and is considered to be a commodity in itself. If a person cuts up a unit (fifty sheets) of plywood and ends up with the equivalent of twenty sheets in scrap, something must be wrong. This may be the result of an operator not paying attention, or perhaps it results from incorrect ordering of material. Remember, most panel products are not only available in 4′×8′ sheets but can be ordered in 4′×10′ sheets, and sometimes 4′×12′ sheets. True, these are special order items, but it may be worth the wait if the square-foot price is the same and you will realize better usage when cutting up a particular job.

Remnants and By-Products

In any woodworking business, material remnants will be generated regardless of how well material usage is planned. This is a fact of life! The key here is to use those remnants in future projects or in some other way whenever possible. Each time a remnant is used in a project, money is saved. My projects are bid on the basis of material required as if I didn't have a stick of wood on hand. Therefore, each customer is paying for the remnants that are produced by his job. This is only fair because I'm not always sure that these remnants can be used, and I also bear the cost of handling, storing or disposing of them. Keeping this in mind, you should organize remnants in a way that makes you aware of what might be used in the future. Keeping track of remnant "inventory" is important for another reason besides saving money. If any of you are like I am, you probably hate to throw away a good piece of material. If we didn't use or dispose of our remnants, we would be completely buried in them before long.

Some other uses for material remnants would be product development, prototypes and speculation work. All these uses can be helpful to any woodworking business in terms of survival and future products. Product development includes all the development of new ideas for production at a later date. Prototypes are models that are built either to scale or actual size for ongoing production concepts. The use of remnants in product development and prototypes will obviously help to offset the cost of those items. Incidentally, prototypes are usually charged to the customers who eventually buy the finished products. Speculation pieces are all products which are produced before there is a market. If our speculative products can be produced by using remnants, then they will become *by-products* of our mainstay business.

> *Each time a remnant is used in a project, money is saved.*

By-products are "gravy" items in any industry, including woodworking. Whenever a product is produced with the waste or remnants of a mainstay business, it is considered to be a by-product. In my business, I often produce turned bowls, lamps, laminated cutting boards and a whole host of other craft items with my remnants. This always does my heart good because number one, I am using precious hardwoods (instead of burning them), and number two, I am turning my scrap into money. Another consideration when a lot of remnants are generated is to "hook up" with someone else who can use your remnants in their business. I have a friend who will buy all of the hardwood plywood remnants I can generate. He uses them to make a line of small display boxes which he sells at fairs. I am doing him a favor buy selling the remants to him, and he is doing me a favor by getting them out of my way. These type of affiliations are real win-win situations!

SHOP SAFETY AND WORKING WITH OSHA AND STATE AGENCIES

There are certain government agencies set up to protect workers from unsafe working conditions or occupational hazards. The Occupational Safety and Health Administration (OSHA), is just that type of agency (see "OSHA's Purpose," p. 75). OSHA is a federally administrated organization within the Deptartment of Labor whose purpose is: ". . . to assure so far as possible every working man and woman in the Nation safe and healthful working conditions and to preserve our human resources." The Occupational Safety and Health Act was passed by a bipartisan Congress in 1970. Until that time, the burden of lost production, lost wages, medical expenses and disability compensation due to unsafe or hazardous working conditions on the nation's commerce was staggering. The general coverage of the Act (OSHAct, Public Law 91-596) extends to all employers and their employees in the fifty states, the District of Columbia, Puerto Rico and all other territories under federal government jurisdiction. Coverage is provided either directly by federal OSHA or through an OSHA-approved state program.

As defined by the Act, an employer is any "person engaged in a business affecting commerce who has employees, but does not include the United States or any state or political subdivision of a state." Therefore, the Act applies to employers and employees in such varied fields as manufacturing, construction, longshoring, agriculture, law and medicine, charity and disaster relief, organized labor, and private education. According to this definition, a woodworking business which has employees is definitely under the jurisdiction of OSHA. Self-employed persons without employees are not covered under OSHA.

As employers in a woodworking business, we are required to comply with the safety standards of both the federal and state government agencies. These agencies are not monsters that are interested only in destroying our businesses. They really are there to help us in the long run. My personal dealings with the people within these agencies has always been pleasant and helpful. For woodworking, OSHA is concerned with such things as machinery guards, dust collection, personal eye and ear protection (safety goggles and

OSHA'S PURPOSE

Under the Occupational Safety and Health Act, the Occupational Safety and Health Administration (OSHA) was created within the Department of Labor to:

- Encourage employers and employees to reduce workplace hazards and to improve existing methods or implement new ways to prevent safety and health problems;
- Provide for research in occupational safety and health to develop innovative ways of dealing with occupational safety and health problems;
- Establish "separate but dependent responsibilities and rights" for employers and employees for the achievement of better safety and health conditions;
- Maintain a reporting and record-keeping system to monitor job-related injuries and illnesses;
- Establish training programs to increase the number and competence of occupational safety and health personnel;
- Develop mandatory job safety and health standards and enforce them effectively; and
- Provide for the development, analysis, evaluation and approval of state occupational safety and health programs.

earplugs) and other safety concerns that we should all employ anyway.

Workplace Inspections

To enforce its standards, OSHA is authorized under the Act to conduct workplace inspections. Every establishment covered by the Act is subject to inspection by OSHA, and inspections are conducted without advance notice. In fact, alerting an employer in advance of an OSHA inspection can bring a criminal fine of up to $1,000 and/or a six month-jail term. Similarly, states with their own occupational safety and health programs can also conduct inspections.

Where to Get Copies of the OSHA Standards

OSHA standards fall into four major categories: General Industry, Maritime, Construction and Agriculture.

A copy of the standards relating to the above categories is available for purchase from the Superintendent of Documents, U.S. Government Printing Office (GPO), Washington, DC, or local offices. The standards are available in hard copy or on a CD-ROM. The telephone number for the Washington, DC, GPO is (202) 512-1800.

CHAPTER SUMMARY

- The "operations" department of a woodworking business is the production shop. The physical layout of a shop is very important when it comes to efficiency. Shop efficiency will quickly translate into time and money saved. The proper placement of the stationary power tools and "flow" of materials through the shop are part of good operating efficiency.

- The "golden triangle" of woodworking machinery includes: the table saw, the jointer and the radial arm saw. These three pieces of equipment should be placed close to each other with the table saw in the middle. The radial arm saw should be placed on the longest wall in the shop. Most of the stationary equipment not included in the golden triangle can be placed against the walls and/or mounted on wheels. The shaper will require distance on all sides of the cutter according to specific operations. To reduce noise and gain floor space, compressors and dust extractors can be mounted outside the shop.

- All tools should be maintained on a "preventive" basis for accuracy, safety and efficiency. A maintenance schedule should be kept for each power tool in the shop. These maintenance schedules should include: all the particulars about the tool, the parts to be maintained and the dates on which the tool was serviced. These maintenance schedules will become a matter of record and should be kept in one place that is convenient to everyone concerned.

- It is far better to start your business with sufficient, affordable equipment, than to go into debt for nonessential, higher-priced items. Upgrading equipment as money will allow is a good approach to equipment ownership. Keeping current with new equipment innovations is a benefit of upgrading. It is wise to consider the used tool market before purchasing a new tool. Maintenance records are useful when selling your used equipment.

- Material storage is a big concern for any type of woodworking operation. Shop floor space is a commodity and is best utilized for operations. Some methods of cost-effective material storage include: under the floor level, loft spaces, horizontal racks, vertical racks and satellite buildings. Under ideal conditions, solid material is best stored flat in a dry space and at floor level. In raised-foundation buildings, if storage is not incorporated within the shop space, material can be stored underneath it. Loft storage can be incorporated when a building has sufficient height. Horizontal and vertical racks are good options for short-term material storage. Depending on the size of the woodworking operation, a satellite storage space may be a good option.

- Whenever possible, finished products should be shipped or delivered immediately after they are finished. Once finished products are delivered, they are no longer your responsibility and the final payment from the customer will be due. When it is necessary to store finished work, it is best to store it somewhere other than the work space. It is important to store finished products safely and for as little expense as possible.

- Production flow refers to the way raw material comes into the shop, is processed, then shipped or delivered. Trimming steps from this production process will save time and money. In the ideal production shop situation, the processing operations would be placed between receiving and shipping doors. If products require the additional step of packaging, this may be best done somewhere other than in the work space. If packaging is done within the work space, the station is best located in the area closest to the shipping operation.

- The material aspect of a bid will often represent one-third of the total price. With that in mind, every cut should be well thought out before it is made. An inexperienced worker can do more harm than good if not properly trained in material usage. To minimize waste, it may be necessary to specify lengths and widths when ordering solid material. For best usage, a panel "cutting" list can be made in advance for $4' \times 8'$, $4' \times 10'$ and $4' \times 12'$ material.

- Material remnants will always be generated in a woodworking business. These remnants can be turned into money by using them in product development, prototypes and speculation work. Whenever a product is produced with waste or remnants of a mainstay product, it is considered to be a by-product. If a company does not use its own by-products, remnants can be sold to other concerns.

- There are certain government agencies set up to protect U.S. workers from unsafe working conditions, or occupational hazards. OSHA is a federally administered organization concerned with safety. As employers in a woodworking business, we are required to comply with the safety standards of both the federal and state government agencies. For the woodworking industry, OSHA is concerned with such things as machinery guards, dust collection, personal eye and ear protection and other safety measures which we should employ anyway. OHSA may conduct workplace inspections without advance notice and has the right to levy fines.

7

Tracking Your Business

In the day-to-day responsibilities of running a business, there are a multitude of details to pay attention to. Tracking the progress of a business is not the least of these details, and if done properly it may indicate some "focus" changes along the way. I have talked a lot about good planning in the previous chapters, and by now, we all know the importance of this. Part of good planning, however, is being willing to "course correct" if necessary. Plans can be altered or amended if market "indicators" dictate that this must be done for the good of the business. These indicators include:

- A drop in sales
- Efficiency problems in the workplace (operations)
- Changes in the marketplace
- Discontented customers
- Problems with material suppliers

> *Plans can be altered or amended if market "indicators" dictate that this must be done for the good of the business.*
>
> ———
>
> *If work quotas seem to fluctuate, something in the operation is inconsistent and must be analyzed.*

These indicators should all be evaluated to help insure the ongoing success of any business. This evaluation can be charted daily and then compiled periodically for analysis. For instance, in the area of inefficiency in the workplace, quotas can be set (see "Work Quota Chart," p. 79). If work quotas seem to fluctuate, something in the operation is inconsistent and must be analyzed. Perhaps there is an employee negatively affecting worker morale on certain days of the week, or perhaps materials are not being delivered on time. Whatever the case may be, if there is a problem that you are *not* aware of and nothing is done about it, the problem will continually "drain" the system.

MEASURING SUCCESS DAY BY DAY

Monitoring business activity can be a full-time effort in itself, but the different aspects of a business (such as sales, operations and accounting) must be kept under control. If the business has more than one person involved (has employees) some of the daily monitoring responsibility can be delegated. There is more than one reason to delegate responsibility. First of all, the job will get done, but more importantly, the employee who is given the responsibility will realize that you are keeping track of things. For instance, in the area of accounting, whoever is responsible for bank deposits should inform the owner each day as to account balances. I have a friend who never paid attention to the daily balances of his company

WORK QUOTA CHART

ITEM: MAPLE CUTTING BOARD

SIZE: 1½″×18″×24″

Daily production quota: 100

Weekly production quota: 500

For the month of: August 1998

Day of Week	Parts Produced	(+ or − quota)
Monday	90	−10
Tuesday	97	−3
Wednesday	112	+12
Thursday	104	+4
Friday	97	−3
Weekly parts:	500	**(+ or −):** 0
Monday	89	−11
Tuesday	104	+4
Wednesday	111	+11
Thursday	97	−3
Friday	102	+2
Weekly Parts:	503	**(+ or −):** +3
Monday	96	−4
Tuesday	103	+3
Wednesday	100	0
Thursday	93	−7
Friday	104	+4
Weekly Parts:	496	**(+ or −):** −4
Monday	103	+3
Tuesday	92	−8
Wednesday	114	+14
Thursday	101	+1
Friday	94	−6
Weekly Parts:	504	**(+ or −):** +4
Monthly Parts:	2003	**(+ or −):** +3

For efficiency in the operations department, work quotas can be set, documented and then compiled for periodic analysis.

accounts and then "paid the price." His accountant was embezzling cash for more than six months before it was noticed. When the accountant was asked why she was so bold, her response was, "I didn't think he cared." Had my friend just paid attention to the deposits each day, this problem would not have occurred.

Each department should have someone responsible and accountable for writing daily reviews in areas like production quotas, materials usage and sales. These reviews can then be compiled and brought to the attention of the owner or board of directors during regularly scheduled meetings (weekly meetings are always a good idea), or informally at a supervisor's request. In any event, it becomes the owner's responsibility to "review the reviews" and implement changes if necessary. This is a system which is known in government as "checks and balances." In businesses which deal with large amounts of money, such as banks and casinos, everybody is checking everybody. Why is a woodworking business any different? Products are money, and if something goes wrong and is not corrected, money as well as jobs may be lost and everybody loses.

> *If the business has more than one person involved (has employees), some of the daily monitoring responsibility can be delegated.*

Tracking business functions on a daily basis does wonders for a business. It also can do wonders for company morale. The ongoing good morale within a business will reflect in the work that is being done. If the appropriate corrections are made along the way as needed, the obvious end result will be improved profits. Nothing makes a business owner happier than ongoing success, and this happiness should be conveyed from the top down so that everyone involved in the success shares in the joy. Most people like to be part of a "winning" team, and a few kind words to the persons responsible for success will help to ensure that the success will continue. Give credit where and when credit is due!

A DROP IN SALES

Sales figures should always be watched closely. A drop in sales is always cause for alarm and should be evaluated immediately. Businesses often have "seasons" when their products typically sell better. Every business concern should compile daily, weekly, and monthly sales records and also institute year-to-year evaluations and comparisons. In the case of a seasonal business, a yearly "track" record should be established after the first year. This track record should then be compared to records in future years for hopeful improvement (see "Yearly Sales of Regional Items," p. 81). Reasons that sales can drop include:

- The particular time of the year
- Discontented customers
- Prices being undercut by competitors
- Lack of good quality control
- The economy

Slipping sales can be rectified if the problem (or problems) are pinpointed in time. By tracking your business on a day-to-day basis with a focus on sales, fluctuations can be spotted and rectified. If dropping sales are due to the time of year (typically from January to March in the woodworking business) or the general economy, additional advertising or promotions may be necessary. This strategy is part of a good marketing plan which was discussed in chapter five. A marketing plan should have a built-in versatility to help cope with the economic fluctuations of the country. No one can foresee the future, but with the daily evaluation of sales you can control the present.

QUALITY CONTROL

One of the biggest reasons for slipping sales that can be blamed directly on the actual business operation is poor quality control. Quality control has to do with the way product quality is monitored. A business with good product quality control is more likely to keep a loyal customer base. There are a lot of things which affect product quality:

- Employees who don't care about product quality
- Poor or substandard materials
- Machinery or tools which are not maintained
- Rushing products to meet unrealistic quotas
- Inadequate facilities for operations

As mentioned earlier in this chapter, all aspects of a business should be monitored on a daily basis. Operations, which is the heart of all business, should be the number one daily concern. For quality control reasons, someone within the operation should be directly responsible for inspecting each and every product before it leaves the shop.

A simple form which pertains to the product being checked can be designed, used and in-

YEARLY SALES OF SEASONAL ITEMS

SEASONAL ITEM:		COST OF PRODUCING ITEM:	
SALES YEAR:		% OF PREVIOUS YEARLY INCREASE:	
BEST SALES MONTHS:		GROSS SALES LAST YEAR:	

MONTH	QUANTITY SOLD	BACK ORDERS	DOLLAR AMOUNT
		GROSS SALES THIS YEAR:	

For a seasonal business or product, a chart for tracking yearly sales can be made for future comparison.

cluded with the product (see "Quality Control Slip," p. 82). If products do slip in quality for any of the reasons listed above, word will spread like wildfire through the customer base. Once a negative opinion of the product reaches customers, it is very difficult to win them back—more difficult in fact than attracting them in the first place. If a poor product does slip through the system and is brought to your attention by any customer, that product should be replaced immediately along with a sincere apology.

TRACKING OPERATIONS EFFICIENCY

Efficiency in the workplace must be an ongoing effort by everyone involved. It is not enough to simply implement good shop efficiency practices (chapter six); these practices must also be monitored and evaluated constantly. Employees and even business owners can sometimes become complacent and lax when not reminded of the business "mission" and company policy. New employees also need to be aware of company policy. For example, regarding remnant usage, they may be inclined to consider the remnants as just "scrap" and either discard or take the remnants home. We all know by now that even sawdust can be sold, and theoretically there is no such thing as scrap (unless the owner says so). Uninformed employees may not be dishonest or want to hurt the company, but they may in fact be affecting the company's "bottom line" profits.

One way to track operations efficiency is to refer to a daily or weekly performance record of operations. This is done with a tracking calendar (see p. 83) which shows production on a daily and weekly basis. This calendar can become the responsibility of whoever is in charge of operations. Regardless of what the product is (breadboards to bars), daily progress should be noted on the calendar. At the end of each week, the weekly column will be used to total the daily figures. These calendars should be kept in chronological order and referred to for future comparisons. If an exceptionally productive week is noted, find out why more work was done during that particular week. Conversely, if a particularly unproductive week is noted, find out why. Of course, things like employees being absent will result in less production, so be careful that you are comparing "apples to apples."

> *For quality control reasons, someone within the operation should be directly responsible for inspecting each and every product before it leaves the shop.*
>
> ———
>
> *Efficiency in the workplace must be an ongoing effort by everyone involved.*

CHANGES IN THE MARKETPLACE

Changes in the marketplace occur every day. These changes can be positive or negative (or a combination of both) to your particular business. If the *negative* changes in the marketplace are not recognized and counteracted in time, they can adversely affect business profits. If positive changes are not recognized or anticipated, the business might not be in a position to cope with increased demand for its product in time to take advantage of the situation. Even

> *If an exceptionally productive week is noted, find out why more work was done during that particular week.*

megacorporations struggle with these concepts every day. In a production business, for instance, it would be appropriate to have an ample stock of product if increased demand is anticipated for any reason. Reasons for changes in the marketplace would include:

- Seasonal demand
- Increased competition
- The condition of the economy
- The opening of new product venues
- Media responses to a product (positive or negative)

Most of these changes can be anticipated if close attention is paid to market indicators such as your daily sales records, news in trade publications, market surveys and current events. Seasonal demand can always be anticipated, but knowing how much demand will be made for a particular product requires specific knowledge. This is where your tracking records and knowledge of current events will come in handy. For instance, if you know from your records that demand for a product has increased a steady 10 percent a year at Christmas time for the last three years, you can plan appropriately. If the media is reporting that a better (or worse) than usual retail sales year is expected due to the economy, this can also be also be taken into consideration.

QUALITY CONTROL SLIP

ITEM: DATE INSPECTED:

THIS PRODUCT HAS BEEN CHECKED AND APPROVED BY:

For a production woodworking business, a quality control slip can be included with the product before shipping.

AUGUST 1998

SUN	MON	TUES	WED	THURS	FRI	SAT
						1
2	**3** work or units completed	**4** work or units completed	**5** work or units completed	**6** work or units completed	**7** work or units completed	**8** total units or work completed
9	**10** work or units completed	**11** work or units completed	**12** work or units completed	**13** work or units completed	**14** work or units completed	**15** total units or work completed
16	**17** work or units completed	**18** work or units completed	**19** work or units completed	**20** work or units completed	**21** work or units completed	**22** total units or work completed
23	**24** work or units completed	**25** work or units completed	**26** work or units completed	**27** work or units completed	**28** work or units completed	**29** total units or work completed
30	**31** work or units completed					

For tracking an operation's efficiency on a daily or weekly basis, a simple calendar should be used, updating and referring to it frequently.

New market venues such as the Internet (see chapter five) are usually given lots of media attention when still in their infancy. If more-than-normal attention is being given to a subject in the media, there must be some merit to it. In other words, "where there is smoke, there is usually fire." Business owners should always pay attention to any mention of new market venues. New market venues may or may not apply to your particular products, but any time they present a chance to increase sales by more than 1 percent, they're worth consideration.

BE WILLING TO CHANGE YOUR PRODUCT FOCUS

When any business has been in existence for a while, demand for a particular product may change. Business owners must be willing to

> *If the negative changes in the marketplace are not recognized and counteracted in time, they can adversely affect business profits.*
>
> ———
>
> *Business owners should always pay attention to any mention of new market venues.*

change their product focus to comply with the demand for that product. Of course, the demand for a specific product can increase or decrease according to market trends, increased competition or new product designs which render old ones obsolete. For instance, during the more than a quarter century that my business has been operating, I have gone through several product phases. During one phase, I was producing a line of rustic furniture because it was in "vogue." During another phase, which lasted five years, I was producing all my products in red oak per customer specifications. The phase that followed immediately after the red oak phase had me producing anything but red oak. Naturally, these were all "evaluations" which were made gradually but consistently over a period of time. When I anticipated that the red oak phase was coming to an end, I no longer purchased this species of wood in quantity, for obvious reasons.

Had I remained rigid in my product design, my business definitely would have suffered along the way. Part of tracking your business is to take note of what is in demand as time goes by. This is done by careful review of past sales and an awareness of competitive products as they enter the market. Where competition is concerned, sooner or later good products are *always* copied. That is the way of the world, and it will always be the case with competition. You may have a "corner" on the mar-

ket for a while, but someone will inevitably come up with a cheaper way to produce that product or do a better job of marketing it.

As a business becomes established (three years minimum), the customer base will grow. This will be a result of the natural compounding effect (see chapter eight) which will occur with good marketing. As this customer base grows, it will become easier to "introduce" new concepts and products. Customers will already know and trust your current products, so they will be more inclined to consider something new by the same manufacturer. For example, I have a friend who started a business which produced multiples of one wooden item which were sold at crafts fairs.

> *Business owners must be willing to change their product focus to comply with the demand for that product.*
>
> ———
>
> *Part of tracking your business is to take note of what is in demand as time goes by.*

Because he had a product that was making money, it was quickly copied, and he had competition. Having anticipated that this would happen, he had begun working on new products which he could sell to his established customers while he was finding new venues (other marketplaces) for his work. He eventually entered the mail order catalog business and compounded his markets manyfold. Because he was not afraid to try new products and look for new markets, his business *evolved* faster than the market was changing. When a business caters to more than one market venue, it can use this "network" to introduce other products.

> *Like a marketing plan,*
> *a business plan should*
> *evolve and develop.*

DEVELOPING YOUR BUSINESS PLAN

When organizing a business plan (see chapter one), a list of projections are made. Once the business is actually in operation, the business plan should "evolve" and develop based on documented information of the operation. An indication of how a business is actually performing will be evident in the information gathered during different forms of tracking.

Information included in the accounting records and daily operations records will influence how a business plan will develop.

Like a marketing plan, a business plan should evolve and develop. Future growth of a business is projected according to past performance which will in turn affect the business plan. If money is needed to expand production of an existing product, a lender or investor will want to see past performance records of that product. Therefore, it is important to keep performance records of production items (see "Monthly Sales Goals," p. 86). As a rule, the use of these records will be twofold. They will first be used in consideration of expansion, and secondly for securing capital.

DISCONTENTED CUSTOMERS OR CLIENTS

We all know what harm discontented customers can do to our businesses. If a business owner

> *Don't be afraid to*
> *ask your customers how*
> *they feel about your employees.*

does not pay attention to "customer reaction" at all times, the worst can happen. Discontent can be born from poor products (quality control) or poor service from representatives of the business. The slogan "The customer is always right" has tremendous merit for all concerned. I have always had a "No questions asked" policy with my business when it comes to the customer being satisfied. It is always better to take a little loss on the product in question than to be "rigid" about a customer complaint and suffer a loss of business in the future. For instance, if a customer complains about unsightly sanding marks in a wooden product, the pieces should either be corrected or replaced without charge.

> *It is always good to have more than*
> *one source for materials and*
> *supplies so that comparisons can be*
> *made from time to time.*

On the service end, everybody who is involved with a business is considered to be a representative of that business. For this reason, good "people skills" among employees must be encouraged by the business owner. People skills as they pertain to business include such things as communication ability, courtesy and concern for the customer. I am sure that we have all encountered a rude or unhappy representative of a business at one time or another. This type of behavior will always reflect on that business even if the ownership itself has a courteous point of view. With all of this in mind, it is important as business owners that we know how our representatives are treating our customers. Don't be afraid to ask your customers how they feel about your employees. Sometimes customers will not let you know how they are being treated until you bring it up.

MONTH: _____

PRODUCT	SALES			INCOME			PER UNIT		
	ESTIMATED	ACTUAL	OVER/UNDER	ESTIMATED	ACTUAL	OVER/UNDER	ESTIMATED	ACTUAL	OVER/UNDER
TOTALS									

For tracking and future expansion purposes, performance records can be kept for a specific product.

MATERIAL SUPPLIERS

Our material suppliers and vendors are all in business just like we are. They have the same basic business concerns to pay attention to, but the way that they run their businesses can directly affect our business. How our suppliers buy their goods and run their operations will dictate the prices we are charged. It is always good to have more than one source for materials and supplies so that comparisons can be made from time to time. If radical price changes are evident from one order to the next, these changes must be questioned. Perhaps a mistake was made by the person that processed the order, or there was a "real" price change that we were not made aware of. Whatever the case may be, the answer is important so that the situation can be evaluated and a correction made if needed.

As business relationships between consumers and suppliers continue, a mutual trust will be developed. If trust is breached on either end, it will definitely affect the business operations of both concerns. Therefore, it is important to treat your suppliers as you wish to be treated. At the same time, "business is business," and as industrial consumers we must keep track of all supplier transactions. Typically, there are three stages, or separate transactions, to every material or supply order:

- An order is placed with a supplier (see "Sample Purchase Order," p. 87)
- The material or supplies are shipped (see "Sample Packing Slip," p. 88)

P U R C H A S E O R D E R

YOUR COMPANY NAME

Address (first line)

Address (second line)

City, Province or State, Postal Code

Phone Number

Fax Number

FOR: Vendor Name

    Address (first line)

    Address (second line)

    City, Province or State

    Postal Code   Country

VENDOR INSTRUCTIONS

ORDERED BY:	PURCHASE ORDER NUMBER:
ORDER DATE:	SHIP VIA:
DATE REQUIRED:	PARTIAL SHIPMENT ALLOWED:
PAYMENT TERMS:	BACKORDERS ALLOWED:

SHIP TO

NAME

COMPANY

ADDRESS

CITY	PROVINCE/STATE
COUNTRY	POSTAL CODE

ITEM NO.	QTY.	ITEM DESCRIPTION	PRICE EACH	TOTAL

	SUB TOTAL:	
TAX RATE: _____	TAX:	
	SHIPPING & HANDLING:	
Include P.O. Number on all invoices and correspondence.	OTHER COSTS:	
Please notify us immediately if this order cannot be filled on time.	TOTAL AMOUNT:	

INTERNAL USE ONLY

ORDERED BY:	DEPARTMENT:
APPROVED BY:	DATE OF APPROVAL:
DATE RECEIVED:	
IN GOOD ORDER:	IF NOT, RESOLVED:
COMMENTS:	

PACKING SLIP

VENDOR COMPANY NAME

Address (first line)

Address (second line)

City, State or Province, Postal Code

Phone Number

Fax Number

SHIP TO: Company name

Address (first line)

Address (second line)

City, State or

Province, Postal

Code

BILL TO: Person or company

Address (first line)

Address (second line)

City, State or

Province, Postal Code

SALESPERSON: _____ DATE OF ORDER: _____

PAYMENT TERMS: _____ DATE ORDER SHIPPED: _____

METHOD OF SHIPMENT: _____ FOB POINT: _____

ORDER NUMBER: _____

ITEM NO.	QTY.	DESCRIPTION	PRICE EACH	AMOUNT

SUBTOTAL: _____

TAX RATE: _____ TAX: _____

SHIPPING AND HANDLING: _____

PREVIOUS AMOUNT OWING: _____

CREDIT: _____

YOU PAY THIS AMOUNT: _____

- The order is received (see "Sample Invoice," p. 89)

These three transactions will each be a separate matter of record, which must be cross-referenced and "balanced" before an order cycle is complete.

It is not uncommon to find discrepancies, due to human error, between the three "order" documents. It is always good policy that the person responsible for ordering materials and supplies communicate with the person responsible for re-

INVOICE

VENDOR COMPANY NAME

Address (first line)
Address (second line)
City, State or Province, Postal Code
Phone Number
Fax Number

SHIP TO: Company name
Address (first line)
Address (second line)
City, State or
Province, Postal
Code

BILL TO: Person or company
Address (first line)
Address (second line)
City, State or
Province, Postal Code

SALESPERSON: _____ DATE OF ORDER: _____

PAYMENT TERMS: _____ DATE ORDER SHIPPED: _____

METHOD OF SHIPMENT: _____ FOB POINT: _____

INVOICE NUMBER: _____ INVOICE DATE: _____

ORDER NUMBER: _____

ITEM NO.	QTY.	DESCRIPTION	PRICE EACH	AMOUNT

SUB TOTAL: _____

TAX RATE: _____   TAX: _____

SHIPPING & HANDLING: _____

PREVIOUS AMOUNT OWING: _____

CREDIT: _____

YOU PAY THIS AMOUNT: _____

ceiving them. This can be done by posting all orders in the receiving department. If this is done, when orders are received they can be checked against packing slips or "tallies" (board footage) and discrepancies will be recognized immediately. I once had a supplier who had a bad habit of consistently sending me 50 percent more lumber than I ordered. Because my foreman was made aware

> *It is always good policy that the person responsible for ordering materials and supplies communicate with the person responsible for receiving them.*

of the board footage amounts of my orders, he was able to discover the errors before the truck left my shop. After a few times of having to haul the extra material back to his yard, the supplier began sending the correct amounts. It is a simple matter of "one hand knowing what the other is doing."

DEALING WITH COMPETITORS

Every business has competition—that's a fact of life. The minute we "let down our guard" as business owners, market share could be lost. Keep a careful eye on your competition at all times. Smart competitors will be watching your business, so it is important to be aware of their market position at any given time. Competitors are not enemies, but they do sometimes help dictate product price ceilings (the most that can be charged) and new product trends. As a rule, I remain friendly with my immediate competitors, and am not afraid to call them to discuss matters that affect my (or their) business. By doing this, I find that they are less inclined to undercut my prices in an effort to remove me as a threat. If a competitor can truly produce a product for less than I can, then there must be something wrong with my operation. Instead of blaming the competitor, it would be more appropriate for me to take a look at what must be done to make my operation more efficient.

How competitors market their products should also be of interest to every business owner. The competition factor is what opens up new markets, expands old markets and dictates product prices.

You can learn a lot about marketing from your competitors. For instance, as I recommended in chapter five, before you set up a Web page, because it is a relatively new market venue, it is a good idea to see how established businesses market themselves. This is not cheating, just good competitive technique. A method that is "tried and proven," unless it is copyrighted or patented, is fair game. The nature of competition and the "free market" is to take a concept, expound upon it and make it better.

> *Keep a careful eye on your competition at all times.*
>
> ———
>
> *Accounting records are valuable for business tracking purposes as well as for taxes.*

ACCOUNTING AND RECORD KEEPING

Good accounting is essential in any business. Accounting as it applies to business is a written record of all transactions to do with business. We are mandated by law to do this for tax purposes, but just as important, it is also a means of tracking our business. Included in accounting are two important records that must be kept: a statement of debits and credits, and a settling or balancing of accounts. These are the money issues which will record the ongoing status of the business. Accounting records are valuable for business tracking purposes as well as for taxes. Business tracking is a by-product of accounting. Some of the information that can be extracted from systematic tracking (per week, month, year) include:

- Profit margin (the percentage of profit to gross revenues)
- Account balances (cash on hand and liability)

- Inventory (material and supplies on hand)
- Product, project performance (when more than one product is produced)
- Debt service (how much the business owes on a fixed basis each month: overhead)
- Accounts receivable (the money that is owed the business)
- Accounts payable (how much the business owes for nonoverhead items)
- Employee issues (days missed, performance, rate of pay)
- Supplier issues (discounting, timeliness, availability of items supplied)

The accounting department may consist of the sole operator of the business or be a separate department in itself. In either event, it is the business owner's responsibility to require that business tracking be a part of the accounting process. This tracking aspect of accounting is separate from the "money" issues, and will have its own records. Tracking records include all other records which are kept only for the business owner's sake, such as:

- Equipment maintenance schedules (see chapter six)
- Performance calendars
- Shop drawings (working drawings of completed projects)

These types of records are all valuable and should be stored for possible future reference after being used for their immediate purpose. As an example, I recently had a call from a client whom I had not seen in years. He was calling about a problem with a project that I had completed twenty years ago. There was an electrical problem with a moving bookcase I had designed and built for him. I was able to find the schematic (which impressed him), and I faxed it to him while his electrician was standing by. The interesting thing was that he called me to do another project for him within a week of the incident; my record keeping paid off.

> *It is important to budget current cash flow and anticipated income.*

Plotting Your Finances

Finances, as discussed in chapter three, must be plotted (or projected) periodically for the future. These projections are a form of budgeting in that they will consider how the money received on accounts will be dispersed. With a lot of businesses (such as mine), money is anticipated and received inconsistently. There is not an even flow from month to month. Depending on how projects are overlapped, actual receivables may be heavier in some months than others. For instance, if I am involved in a major project which is all-consuming for three months, that may be my only source of revenue for that time period. While nearing the end of that commitment, I will begin to take deposits on the next project or projects. It is important to budget current cash flow and anticipated income. However the cash flow is anticipated, it is important to "plot" how this money will be used.

Regardless of how income is deposited, distribution should be considered in advance for many reasons. Just like the work load, a current monthly budget should be designed that considers categories such as:

- Regular monthly debt service
- Scheduled repairs and maintenance
- Upgrading and new acquisition of equipment
- Expansion
- Quantity buying of materials

These expenses should be considered in advance so as to not "overextend" the business finances.

In the case of project deposits for custom shops, these should be reserved for the material involvement of that specific order. If money is taken in advance as a down payment on an order to be started in the future, that is where the money should be allocated. When bidding or estimating a job (see chapter four), the material involvement of the given project will be predetermined and the cost will be taken from the down payment (or material deposit) aspect of the contracted amount. One simple way to handle these down payments is to use a separate checking account just for material deposits. By doing this, all of the activity of that account can be monitored as a sort of escrow, or trust, account.

FINDING AND THEN DEALING WITH EMPLOYEES

As I am sure you realize by now, the success or failure of a business is governed by many variables. Employees are by no means the least of these variables. How a business is conducted in day-to-day operations by any of its representatives all adds up somehow in the final analysis. I marvel at the fact that some employers believe that they can put someone in charge of their investment and then simply walk away. As far as I am concerned, nothing could be further from the truth. No one will watch your investment the way you would (or should). Having said all that, I would now like to focus on the subject of dealing with employees.

I am often asked how I go about finding good, loyal and honest employees. This is a fair question which I have no problem answering. Because I have such a client-oriented custom woodworking business, my employees must eventually feel the same way that I do about a lot of things. Attention to detail, respect for clients and a basic love of woodwork are just a few of the things that are important to my business. The way I feel, it really doesn't matter how old a person is or if they have a great deal of experience, as long as they are willing to learn my style of operating. In my business, I call my employees in the operations department "apprentices." For the most part, apprentices are people who are willing to learn for the right reasons. The hope is that they will perpetuate my trade by training apprentices of their own some day. I feel that quality woodworking is a dying art, and this is my little contribution to the future of this art form. I realize that this is not every business owner's dream for his employees, nor is it the dream of every employee, but it is what works for me.

When searching for the right person, I place an ad in my local newspaper under the help wanted section of the classifieds. The ad states that I am seeking a furniture maker's apprentice, and asks that an *informal* resume be sent to a post office box which is listed in the ad. Every time I have run this ad, I receive many letters, which means there are a lot of people willing to learn my trade. By having the correspondence sent to the post office box, I eliminate the possibility of having multitudes descending upon my shop. Being able to review the applicants in a relaxed atmosphere and at my convenience also gives me the time to carefully study the resumes individually. What I look for is how the applicants respond to the position. By asking for an informal resume I am putting the applicant at ease, and at the same time I can note how they respond. It is amazing how much can be learned from a letter. Is the letter neat? Does the applicant ramble on about how good he is? What are the person's reasons for wanting the job? All of these observations will help me form an opinion of the applicant early on. After refining the letters down to three or four prospects, I then arrange the interviews.

This particular method of finding employees is not unique except for the fact that I am not particularly interested in qualifications. Some of my best employees have been persons without a lot of previous woodworking experience. If the candidate is honest, willing to learn and intelligent, I can work with that. Once a candidate

> *Trust works both ways;*
> *it is important that*
> *your employees trust you.*

is hired, it is time to start building a rapport. Trust works both ways; it is important that your employees trust you. If employees respect you and feel that you care about them as people, they will do their best job. On the other hand, if they do not respect you, they will take advantage of their position, or simply quit. For example, I am aware of a large woodwork production company (twenty employees) that has an employee turnover rate of 80 percent a year. The owner has a bad habit of yelling at and belittling his workers. The workers resent this and either leave for another job or are fired because they don't put forth their best effort.

CHAPTER SUMMARY

- Good procedures of tracking business progress may indicate some "focus" changes. Business plans can be altered or amended if market indicators dictate that this must be done for the good of the business. Business evaluation can be charted daily and then compiled periodically for analysis. By delegating some of the daily business tracking to others, you will make them more responsible.

- Sales figures should always be watched closely. In the case of a seasonal business, a yearly track record should be established after the first year. A marketing plan should have a built-in versatility to help cope with the economic fluctuations of the country.

- One of the biggest reasons for slipping sales that can be blamed directly on the actual business operation is poor quality control. Operations, the heart of all business, should be the

number one daily concern. Once a "negative" opinion of a product reaches customers, it is very difficult to win those customers back.

- Efficiency at the workplace must be an ongoing effort by everyone involved. If new employees are not aware of your company policy, they may take a lot for granted. Regardless of what the product is, daily progress should be noted on a calendar. If an exceptional week is noted, find out why more work was done during that week.

- Both positive and negative changes occur every day in the marketplace. Marketplace changes can be anticipated if close attention is paid to market indicators such as daily sales records, news in trade publications, market surveys and current events. Business owners should always pay attention to new market venues.

- Business owners must be willing to change their product focus to comply with the demand for that product. Reviewing records of past sales will help them anticipate demand for a product. As a business becomes established the customer base will grow. As the customer base grows, it becomes easier to introduce new products. When a business caters to more than one market venue, it will have what is known as a marketing "network."

- How well a business is actually performing will be evident in the information gathered by daily tracking records. Future growth is projected according to past product performance which may affect a developing business plan.

- Business owners should pay attention to "customer reaction" at all times. Customer discontent can be caused by poor products or poor service. It is better to take a loss on a returned product than to suffer a loss of business in the future. Everybody who is involved with a business is a representative of that business. Only professional behavior is acceptable when dealing with customers.

- Material suppliers are in business and have the same basic business concerns as we do. Treat your suppliers as you wish to be treated. How suppliers run their business affects the prices they can charge. If unusual price changes in materials or supplies become evident, they must be questioned. As materials and supplies arrive, the packing slip or tallies must be checked against the order slips.

- Every business has competition which helps to dictate product price ceilings and new product trends. If an immediate competitor can truly produce a product for less than you can, you should pay attention to the efficiency of your operation. Competition opens new markets and expands old markets.

- Good accounting is essential in any business.

A statement of debits and credits and a settling or balancing of accounts must be kept for accounting reasons and can also be used for tracking your business. It is the business owner's responsibility to require that business tracking be a part of the accounting process.

- Finances must be plotted or projected periodically for the future. Financial plotting is a form of budgeting. Anticipating cash flow will ensure that a business does not overextend itself. A separate checking account can be used as an escrow account for deposit of product down payments which are to be used for material and supply acquisition.

- Employees are one of the most important variables in any business. If the candidate for employment is honest, willing to learn and intelligent, experience may not be an important issue. If employees respect a business owner, they will do their best job.

8

Attitude and Working With People

A good personal attitude is an "intangible" ingredient that can mean everything to the success of a business. Attitude refers to a person's mental or emotional state or mood which influences the way that person feels, thinks or acts. Attitude is a very profound subject when you think about how it can affect our daily lives and business dealings. The effects of personal attitude can be either positive or negative, and can make a great deal of difference when we go to the bank. As business owners, how we relate to our customers, employees, suppliers and any other people involved will determine the attitude of the entire business entity.

I have saved this chapter for last for more than one reason, but it is by no means the least important part of this book. Now that the financial, operational and general interworkings of a good woodworking business have been explored, it is time for me to loosen up and talk about my favorite part, the "soul" of a business. I have seen a lot of woodworking concerns come and go due to an owner's bad attitude. The owner may not have started out with a negative attitude,

> *As business owners, how we relate to our customers, employees, suppliers, and any other people involved will determine the attitude of the entire business entity.*

but somewhere along the line that person lost sight of his original intent or "mission." A lot of factors (i.e. mounting materials costs, slumping sales) can change a business owner's attitude if a positive focus is not kept each day. A good attitude is good business, and will be reflected in:

- The quality of the products
- The attitude of the employees
- Customer goodwill
- Supplier goodwill
- Investor and lender cooperation

GOODWILL AND THE COMPOUNDING EFFECT

When an existing (minimum of three years old) business is offered for sale, a percentage of the price is based upon "goodwill." Goodwill for business purposes is the commercial advantage of any business due to its:

- Established popularity
- Reputation
- Patronage
- Advertising
- Location, etc.

These commercial "intangible" advantages are over and above the tangible business assets. Goodwill is a salable item (which is actually spelled out in business sales contracts—see "Agreement for the Sale of a Business," p. 96) and can represent as much as 50 percent of the selling price of a business. What this means is that, while

AGREEMENT FOR THE SALE OF A BUSINESS

DATE _____, 19 _____

RECEIVED FROM _____

THE SUM OF _____ DOLLARS

AS PART PAYMENT FOR THE FOLLOWING DESCRIBED _____ BUSINESS SITUATED

IN COUNTY OF_____ STATE OF _____

REAL ESTATE VALUE (IF APPLICABLE): $_____

INTERIOR IMPROVEMENTS (IF APPLICABLE): $_____

BUSINESS RELATED FIXTURES (IF APPLICABLE): $_____

GOODWILL (WHEN A BUSINESS IS OVER 3 YEARS OLD): $_____

THE ENTIRE PRICE TO BE PAID FOR SAID ABOVE DESCRIBED _____ PROPERTY

IS _____ DOLLARS

($_____), PAYABLE AS FOLLOWS:

TITLE TO BE PERFECT _____ DEED TO BE EXECUTED

AND DELIVERED BY THE SAID TITLE CO. _____

ON OR BEFORE THE _____ DAY OF _____, 19_____, PROVIDED,

HOWEVER, THAT SUM OF $_____

IS PAID AT SAID DATE; BUT IF SAID SUM IS NOT PAID ON OR BEFORE THE SAID _____

DAY OF _____, 19 _____ THEN THIS CONTRACT IS TO BE OF NO EFFECT, AND IN THAT EVENT THE SUM OF

$ _____ IS TO BE RETAINED BY

_____

SIGNATURE OF SELLER _____

SIGNATURE OF BUYER _____

Goodwill is a salable item, which is actually spelled out in business sales contracts.

building tangible assets for the business, a company or corporation is also building the additional intangible asset of goodwill. That intangible business asset is directly related to how the business is being operated and can be projected for the future. For example, if a business has a track record of doubling its sales for three years in a row, the assumption can be made that given the same practices it will also double in the fourth year. If this business is sold before the fourth year, there will be a "goodwill" dollar amount which can be added to the sales price which anticipates that sales will double according to the trend.

The established popularity, reputation and patronage (goodwill) of a business are all governed by the attitude of the owner(s). If business is conducted in less than a professional manner, the company is not likely to grow in the area of goodwill.

> *The established popularity, reputation and patronage (goodwill) of a business are all governed by the attitude of the owner(s).*

On the other hand, if business is conducted professionally, and there is an overall good attitude present, the company will flourish according to the extent of that good attitude. Starting at the top (with the owner or owners), the effects of a good business attitude will compound as the attitude is made a matter of policy throughout the business and is extended to its customers. For instance, the attitude (supported by consequent action) that business should be a "win-win" situation for both the seller and buyer will make both parties happy. If the buyers (customers) leave your establishment as "winners" they will be sure to tell their friends. The friends will then repeat the process and the effects of the original sales experience will be compounded exponentially.

> *How a business "presents" itself and its products to the public is a part of being professional.*

The "professional" manner in which a business is conducted should extend through all of its many aspects. This would include: all operations, presentations and advertising policies, and the general demeanor of the entire business. For instance, the operations department should be conducted safely, efficiently, neatly and courteously by all involved. In larger companies this professional attitude is conveyed through a "chain of command" which begins with the owners or directors and is carried throughout the business down to the persons with the least seniority or responsibility. Any department which is not conducted with a professional attitude will adversely affect all the other departments which make up the business. For example, a production facility with a high incidence of safety violations and accidents will cost the company more than money. The reputation of that facility will be less than satisfactory, and employee morale will not be good. Bad morale results in a "negative" attitude which will filter through all departments of a business and cause dissent among the employees.

PRESENTATION

How a business "presents" itself and its products to the public is a part of being professional. Building a professional establishment can help propel a business to success. Professionalism comes naturally to some, but most of us have to work at it. Professionalism is one of those attitudes that must be cultivated by all who are involved in the business. Presentation of any business includes all its visual aspects and the manner in which they are presented:

1. The signage and product packaging must be professional in appearance.
2. The establishment itself should always be clean and maintained in compliance with government rules and regulations.
3. Anyone who represents the business should be presentable, courteous and knowledgeable about the business at hand.
4. Advertising should always be done in a professional manner which is ethical and accurately represents the product being advertised.
5. The business as a whole should always follow through with its commitments in the most efficient and timely manner possible.

> *Business signs and company logos are a form of advertising and should be presented in a consistent and professional manner.*
>
> ———
>
> *It is very important to have a professional "ambiance" associated with all business facilities.*

Professional Signage

The term "signage" is used by architects, planners and designers to refer to all the visual exterior and interior signs used to present a business and its products or services. A lot of signage used by businesses on the exteriors of their establishments is mandated by codes and uniformity restrictions. This is done in an effort to keep all the business signs in a given location professional and consistent with each other in terms of style, size, color, height, etc. Cities, shopping centers, etc. that do not have signage codes will encourage an inconsistent, confusing and unprofessional presentation. For example, cities that have signage codes and restrictions are always more pleasant and easier to traverse. Cities without these codes or restrictions always have a "seedy" look about them, and as a result are uninviting to public commerce (retail).

Business signs and company logos are a form of advertising and should be presented in a consistent and professional manner. If this is done, in time there will be a direct positive association between the professional presentation of the company signs and logo and the reputation of the business itself. A company could in fact produce the best product on the market, but as a result of unprofessional or inconsistent signs/advertising, never reach its full sales potential.

There is a compounding effect of presentation consistency which will in itself help sell products. For instance, there is a positive attitude associated with certain expensive brands of furniture that have a consistent professional presentation. These brands of furniture will sell better than other less expensive brands because "product quality" is presumed by recognition of the company name (see "Sample Business Stationery," p. 99).

The Business Premises

The condition of the actual business premises reflects the attitude of its owners. It is very important to have a professional "ambiance" associated with all business facilities. If business premises are not organized in compliance with codes, or are unprofessional in any way, a negative inference can be made by clientele. This is a fact of human nature when it comes to spending money. If potential customers walk into a business establishment and are offended in any way by what they see, they may be hesitant to buy the products. This may be a negative psychological reaction even if the person likes the product itself. For this reason, a professional establishment should do everything it can to make its patrons comfortable.

Some production businesses may never be visited by the actual end users of their products, but agents from business-oriented entities such as OSHA, insurance companies, wholesale buyers, and lenders may want to see the premises. If any of these agents don't like what they see, it could have a negative effect on the the business. For example, I know of a situation where a business owner was applying for a loan to expand his operation. He "jumped through all the hoops" required to secure the loan. All the initial qualifications were met and the loan seemed to be "in the bag." While the owner was waiting for the deal

 1234 Main St.
Anytown, OH 45207

1234 Main St.   (513) 555-1212
Anytown, OH 45207   (513) 555-2121 FAX

1234 Main St.   plane-n-simple@plane-n-simple.com   (513) 555-1212
Anytown, OH 45207   (513) 555-2121 FAX

Business signage, stationery, cards or any vehicle which is used to advertise a business should be presented in a consistent and professional manner.

to close, however, the bank manager made an impromptu visit to the shop. Apparently appalled by what he saw, the bank manager reported the owner to the city's building department which cited him for several violations. The existing establishment was promptly "red tagged" (closed down) until the code violations were corrected. This cost the business owner a week of operations, a re-evaluation of the loan application and a lot of embarrassment.

The Representatives of a Business

All persons employed by a business are representatives of that business. This includes everyone who communicates in any way—in person, by telephone, fax or E-mail—on behalf of a business. This is an important fact considering that, if not trained properly, one employee could bring down a whole company or corporation. The most obvious case that comes to mind is the commodities broker in Singapore who recently leveraged one of the oldest and largest banks in the world right out of business. He was an employee and representative of the bank, which made the bank liable for his actions. This case is extreme and has nothing to do with a woodworking business other than the fact that both types of business concerns employ people. In other words, the owners of a business are responsible for the actions of their employees while they are on duty.

There is a certain amount of basic screening that should be done before hiring any employee. Honesty, loyalty and good attitude are some of the attributes which would be important in an employee. As stated in chapter seven, these attributes

There is a certain amount of basic screening that should be done before hiring any employee.

are sometimes more important than experience if the person is willing to learn. I would much rather have an employee who knows very little about woodworking but will not "steal me blind," than an employee who "knows it all" but is dishonest. Once a qualified person is hired, he should be trained extensively in the ways of the business. An emphasis on the *attitude* of the business in dealing with customers, suppliers and other employees should be highlighted in the training.

When more than one person is involved with a business, it is important to have a "chain of command" in place.

In business, the owner or any one who represents the owner must follow through with all commitments.

FOLLOWING THROUGH WITH BUSINESS COMMITMENTS

Once employees are released to the affairs of the business (sales, operations, accounting, etc.), they will be speaking as representatives of the business. As a result, any commitments that are made by employees are binding on the company. When more than one person is involved with a business, it is important to have a "chain of command" in place (see "Chain of Command," p. 101). This means that each person will be responsible to someone who is higher up in the company until the "chain" reaches the owner or owners who are ultimately responsible. With this system in place, it is less likely that someone will make a commitment for the company that cannot be honored.

In business, the owner or any one who repre-

CHAIN OF COMMAND

OWNER

OFFICE MANAGER	SALES MANAGER	OPERATIONS MANAGER

Reception	Payroll	Receiving	Shipping	Receiving	Shipping

Accounting	Shop Employees	Shop Employees

Regardless of the size of the business, if there is a "chain of command," it is less likely that someone will make a commitment for the company that cannot be honored.

sents the owner must follow through with all commitments. This diligence is expected of professionals and their organizations. Many a court case has been won by a plaintiff who was treated in less than a professional manner during the course of a business transaction. The customer is usually right when it is learned that there was misrepresentation by a business owner. Misrepresentation in business can be anything from a broken promise to delivery of a substandard product. For this reason, it is important that all transactions be in writing. Verbal commitments, although binding, can be distorted in a way that suits either party. Making all transactions a matter of record will eliminate the possibility of any confusion. For example, if you verbally promise that something will be done in *about* two weeks, all that might be remembered by the customer is the "two weeks." It is far better to write down the exact commitment and retain a copy for yourself for future reference.

> *When estimating the time needed to fulfill a commitment, it is wise to allow yourself more time than will actually be required.*

The "bottom line" with all business commitments is that they should be handled in as timely a manner as possible, and "sooner" not later than promised if possible. This is to the benefit of the business as much as it is the other party. If a business builds a reputation that it "honors" its commitments, people will be less reluctant to enter into transactions with that business. For example, when estimating the time needed to fulfill a commitment, it is wise to allow yourself more time than will actually be required. There is a twofold reason for allowing yourself this leeway. First, the extra time will allow for any unforeseen dilemmas in completing the commitment. In the business world, and especially with woodworking, there are a lot of variables in timetables and money matters that can affect a project. The second reason for allowing extra time is that in the event the business resolves the commitment early, it will make the business *look good*. This is a far better approach than coming up short and having to explain yourself on behalf of the business.

KEEPING CUSTOMERS HAPPY

It is very important to keep your most loyal customers happy. As explained in the section "Getting Repeat Business and Referrals," p. 55, loyal customers are the best source of repeat and referral business. By building a "win-win" situation between the business and good customers, an unbeatable combination will exist. The most loyal customers or clients of a particular business deserve something extra. Large corporations may offer bonus clubs, frequent flyers awards or hotel preferred-customer awards with this concept in mind. In any business these types of programs should always be initiated because of sincere gratitude toward the customer. In my business, I take it upon myself to show my gratitude by giving my special clients something personal that I have made. These are not high-dollar items by any means, but the customer always feels that it is the thought that counts.

> *It is very important to keep your most loyal customers happy.*

A loyal customer is anyone who patronizes your business more than one time. These customers should be treated as family and made to feel welcome each time they are encountered, regardless of what else may be happening at the moment. That is not to say you have to give them presents every time you see them, but once a relationship has been established, these customers should at least receive attention from everyone in your employ. This special treatment will make them feel that you do appreciate their business and are aware of their continued patronage.

PERSONAL DISCIPLINE

Part of working for yourself is the freedom that it allows you to name your own hours. False! When in business, at least in the beginning, no statement could be further from the truth. Those who feel as if going into business will release them from the rigors of punching a clock will soon find

out different. True, going into business is gratifying in most respects, but freedom to do what you please is not one of the perks. Quite the contrary! When starting a business, if done correctly, countless hours will be spent developing a business plan, laying the groundwork to execute the plan, and then actually developing the plan by "hanging out a shingle" and opening the doors for business. When asked how it feels to be in business for myself and name my own hours, I always reply, "Just Great! I only have to work half days, and I get to choose which half I want to work—the first twelve hours or the second twelve hours." This may sound silly, but it is the truth if the business is to run the way that I want it to.

Personal discipline is definitely a key ingredient when entering into business. Without good personal discipline, it is very easy to "stray" and get behind on the workload. Remember, when a business is starting from scratch, there will be no one else responsible for all the particulars involved in that business but the owner. Personally, I devote a minimum of three hours a day just to doing bookwork and staying on top of the business situation. This time, added to the forty hours a week that I spend in actual operations, is more than a full schedule. "How did you write this book?" you might ask. Simple: I did it in all the time I had left over. In spite of the demands, being in business is very gratifying, and believe it or not, I wouldn't trade it for the world.

Having the discipline to report to work everyday and do your best job is born from being organized, committed and responsible. All three of these traits must be cultivated until they become a matter of habit. Thus, the term "good work habits" means that a person is disciplined in work habits. All personal disciplines are a matter of having a focus and then following through with that focus in an efficient and timely manner. For example, if you say you are going to complete a project by a certain date, focus on that date and follow through with the promise. Business owners must "set the pace" of a company by projecting the willingness to focus on the business at hand. The commitment to develop good discipline is very important to the future of a business. A simple way to focus on the "discipline" that it takes to complete a task is by the use of calendar sheets (see "Sample Project Calendar Sheet," p. 104). By posting a calendar which has a specific schedule already outlined, you are reminding yourself of the task at hand. I call this method "self-imposed discipline" and it has always worked for me.

Having the discipline to report to work everyday and do your best job is born from being organized, committed and responsible.

Business owners must "set the pace" of a company by projecting the willingness to focus on the business at hand.

Once customers or clients realize that your company's word is its bond, they will continue to patronize your business and then begin to tell others about their good experiences. Good personal discipline also extends to many other areas of running a business.

- **Discipline with finances**—not overextending the finances, and paying bills on time
- **Discipline with personal temperament**—not overreacting in anger towards others involved in the business
- **Discipline of character**—always setting an example with character decisions (right from

wrong), so that business associates will know what to expect of you
- **Discipline with all business goals and commitments**—following through with all goals and commitments until they are resolved in a timely manner

When you display your best accomplishments, confidence in your work will be reinforced by clients, customers and all who see it.

DEVELOPING CONFIDENCE IN YOUR WORK

Knowing who you are as a woodworker plays a big part in the development of a good business attitude. If you are proud of your work, and that is part of the reason that you entered into business, be *aware* of that pride. Woodwork is an art form and a noble way to make a living. It is important to keep reminders of your best work close at hand and available for all to see. Photographs, newspaper articles, degrees and awards are all "certificates of merit," and should be on display. This is not being egotistical, it is being proud of what you and your business have been involved in. With these displays you also remind yourself of the goals that your business has worked hard to accomplish. When you display your best accomplishments, confidence in your work will be reinforced by clients, customers and all who see it. For example, in the operations part of my business I display an array of photographs and media publications about my work (see p. 105). When clients or other individuals come in, they see the photos and articles

MARCH 1998

SUN	MON	TUES	WED	THURS	FRI	SAT
1	**2** Order all materials	**3** Lay out entire project	**4** Begin the sleeper bases	**5** Pre-cut plywood parts	**6** Pre-cut solid parts	**7** Pre-cut solid parts
8	**9** Pre-cut solid parts	**10** Assemble cabinet cases	**11** Assemble cabinet cases	**12** Assemble face frames	**13** Assemble drawers	**14**
15	**16** Mill all door parts	**17** Assemble cabinet doors	**18** Sand cabinets	**19** Sand doors and drawers	**20** Pre-stain all parts	**21**
22	**23** Pre-finish all parts	**24** Pre-finish all parts	**25** Install all hardware	**26** Hand finish cabinet doors and drawers	**27** Deliver all cabinet parts	**28**
29	**30** Install cabinets	Complete the installation				

A simple way to focus on the "self-discipline" that it takes to complete a project is by using calendar sheets which list a specific project's intended schedule.

on the wall, and often they'll place a product order as a direct result of my display. Making a sale is nice when it happens, but I always receive compliments on the display and that boosts my confidence.

If you are confident about your work and the products your company produces, it will be easy for you to sell. If you have a positive attitude about your products it will be natural for you to want people to own them. On the other hand, if clients or customers sense a lack of your personal confidence in your products, they may hesitate to buy. Confidence is a developed "virtue" which comes with experience. The more you accomplish, the more confident you will become. Each time you complete a project or order, you will be

It is helpful to display photographs, awards or media coverage of products or the company. This helps remind everyone of the successes of the business.

confident that you can do it again, and even do it better the next time. What may seem to be an insurmountable task the first time will become a matter of routine in the future.

WORKING WITH OTHERS

How we relate to other people in the workplace will affect the future of the business. The demeanor of the "boss" can affect a business in either a positive or negative way. If business associates like the owner's manner of dealing with issues, they will not mind presenting their concerns in an honest way. On the other hand, if an owner is known to be a "hot head," associates will be reluctant to present issues truthfully. If you as a business owner are having a bad day, it is difficult to not let it "spill over" into other business matters. If you're in a bad mood, it would be far better to leave the premises for a period of time than to have a problem compounded by a bad attitude. For example, I recently worked with a project manager who

had the bad habit of taking his personal problems out on everyone. As a result, contractors were reluctant to work with him and the project experienced many delays. Believe it or not, this project manager was the representative of a construction company who was responsible for cost effectiveness.

As business owners, the ability to focus on each business issue separately is another "cultivated" discipline. Much more can be accomplished in a day's time by dealing with business issues as they come, separate and apart from any unrelated issues. By categorizing business issues into separate "segments," it is easier to deal with them appropriately. For instance, if you received a call first thing in the morning informing you that you were not awarded a certain contract, that would be disturbing. The second call of the day might be an employee who is reporting that he will be an hour late because his car would not start. These are two totally separate negative issues which are unre-

> *The more you accomplish, the more confident you will become.*
>
> ---
>
> *How we relate to other people in the workplace will affect the future of the business.*

lated. There would not be much sense in getting angry at the employee, who did the right thing by calling, just because you learned earlier that you lost the contract. Who knows—the third call of the day might be someone calling to tell you that you just won the lottery.

LOOKING AND ACTING PROFESSIONAL

Physical appearance can influence business relationships. How you and your employees look and

> *Much more can be accomplished in a day's time by dealing with business issues as they come, separate and apart from any unrelated issues.*
>
> ---
>
> *How you and your employees look and act is a direct reflection on the business.*

act is a direct reflection on the business. Neatness and personal grooming are variables which we have complete control over. An untidy appearance can be a negative and offensive issue that may get in the way of the business at hand. This is the reason a lot of businesses require uniforms or dress codes for their employees who deal with the public. Personal appearance is a part of the business presentation that is designed to make clients or customers feel comfortable. While there is an absolute difference between working in the shop and going out to meet the public, as a business owner you will set the example for your associates. If the owner comes to work with a "five o'clock shadow" every morning, it will be regarded as acceptable, and you will have no recourse in correcting your employees.

Acting in a professional manner should be a requirement for all who are involved with a business. An unprofessional presentation by a business owner or his representatives can "kill" a deal before it gets off of the ground. First impressions are important and can affect business relationships in either a positive or negative way. Until a client gets to know the people personally involved with a business, he or she will rely upon their first impression. If the first im-

pression is negative, that person may *never* get to know the people involved. Professionalism includes:

- **Personal appearance**—Always look presentable.
- **Timeliness**—Always be on time for appointments and honor business commitments.
- **Manners**—Always be polite and courteous to everyone.
- **Assistance**—Always be concerned for people. Even if your business cannot help them, it is wise to give customers references to other sources.
- **Knowledge**—Always have a good grasp of your business and the industry.

The Way You Think

Our thoughts will always be manifested in our actions. The way that we think is usually evident in our appearance, business dealings, organizational skills, goals and personal demeanor. There are a multitude of books available on the subject of "positive thinking," and there is basis in fact to all of them. If your prevailing thoughts are that you are going to be successful, you will be. If you think that you are doomed to failure, you will be. By thinking positive thoughts, you are in essence "projecting" positive behavior. This is especially true when positive thinking is coupled with good planning. Thinking is always the first step to formulating a plan of any kind. In other words, all great plans originate with ideas, and then the plans are executed to a final result.

No person should enter into business without first visualizing success. Even with the many "hurdles" one must overcome and the inevitable setbacks that occur along the way, positive thoughts *must* be kept front and forward in the business owner's mind. There are many levels of success in business, such as conceiving the ideas, executing the ideas and then moving on to bigger

> *Our thoughts will always be manifested in our actions.*
>
> ———
>
> *How you are perceived by people has everything to do with success.*

challenges. Once completed, each one of these accomplishments is a success in itself. Remember, making money is not the only thing that constitutes success. True, making money is the reason that most people go into business, but money will only be the end result of *successful* thinking, organizing, producing and marketing.

A CLOSING STORY

While I was beginning this chapter, a man came to my front door. This person was a complete stranger, his hair was dyed kind of orange, he looked dirty and unkempt (first impression), and he looked down at the ground as he spoke. He explained to me that he had come to town for a job interview and was going to catch a bus back home within the hour. He went on to tell me that he didn't get the job, and didn't understand the reason because he felt that he was as qualified as the next person.

The bus fare was five dollars and he didn't have a cent. He didn't appear to have been drinking or seem otherwise deranged, so I believed his story. Because he was about the same age as my son (about 23), I couldn't help but feel empathetic about his situation. He wanted to know if I could loan him the money, and he would come back and work it off next time he was in town. Naturally, after sensing his desperation I gave him the money, and because he was from out of town, I told him not to worry about paying it back. He thanked me, and said he wished that someone would do something nice for me sometime. A few minutes after I said good-bye, I realized that *he* had just done something nice for me. He made me realize the point of this important chapter. How you are perceived by people has everything to do with success.

Success not only in business but as a person living in the real world is governed by all the basic issues covered in this chapter. Please don't get me wrong about hardships and circumstances that can make a person desperate; I understand that it could happen to anyone, including me. My point is that this *young* man was just fine physically and mentally, but it appeared that he did not think much of himself. He was unkempt and dirty, was an obvious nonconformist (orange hair), and was looking down at his feet as he spoke. When he spoke he seemed to be a nice and sincere person, but the reason for his difficulty in finding a job was obvious. The very unfortunate thing is that somehow he didn't realize that his hardship was self-imposed. Upon reflection, I wished that I could somehow have let him know.

CHAPTER SUMMARY

- A good personal attitude is an "intangible" ingredient which can mean everything to the success of a business. A lot of factors can change a business owner's attitude if a positive focus is not kept each day. A good attitude is reflected in product quality, employee attitude, customer goodwill, supplier goodwill and investor and lender cooperation.
- When an existing business is offered for sale, a percentage of the price is based upon goodwill. Goodwill is the commercial advantage of a business due to its established popularity, reputation, patronage, advertising and/or location. Goodwill is a salable item which can represent as much as 50 percent of the sales

price. If a business is conducted in less than a professional manner, it is not likely to grow in the area of goodwill.

- Building a professional establishment can help propel a business to success. Professionalism is one of those attitudes which must be cultivated by all who are involved in the business. Presentation of any business includes all its visual aspects and the manner in which they are presented.

- The term signage is used by architects, planners and designers to refer to all the visual exterior and interior signs used to present a business and its products or services. Locations that do not have signage codes will encourage inconsistent and confusing presentations. With consistent signage there will be a direct association between the business and the company logo. Poor presentation will limit sales because ongoing name and logo association is not made.

- The condition of the actual business premises reflects the attitude of its owners. If business premises are not organized, in compliance with codes, or unprofessional in any way, a negative inference can be made by clientele.

- All persons employed by a business are representatives of that business. The owners of a business are responsible for the actions of their employees while they are on duty. Honesty, loyalty and good attitude are some of the most important attributes in an employee. Once a qualified person is hired, he should be trained extensively in the company's point of view and attitude in all its dealings.

- Once employees are released to the affairs of the business, they will be speaking as representatives of that business. With a chain of command, each person will be responsible to someone who is higher up in the company. It is important to follow through with all commitments, and that all transactions be in writing. Business commitments should be handled in as timely a manner as possible.

- Loyal customers are the best source of repeat and referral business. The most loyal customers or clients deserve something extra out of gratitude for their business. This special treatment in itself will make them feel that you do appreciate their business and are aware of their continued patronage.

- Those who feel that going into business will release them from the rigors of punching a clock will soon find out different. Personal discipline is a key ingredient when entering into business. Discipline is born from being organized, committed and responsible. All personal disciplines are a matter of having a focus and then following through with that focus in an efficient and timely manner. A self-imposed discipline is a good way to stay committed.

- It is important to keep reminders of your best work close at hand and available for all to see. This will remind you of goals that your company has worked hard to accomplish. If you are confident about your work or the products which your company produces, it will be easy for you to sell. Confidence is a developed virtue which comes with experience.

- The demeanor of a business owner will have a positive or negative effect on the entire company. The ability to focus on each business issue separately is a cultivated discipline. By categorizing business issues into separate unrelated segments, it is easier to deal with them appropriately.

- Physical appearance can influence business

relationships. Neatness and personal grooming are variables which we have complete control over. As a business owner you will set the example for all of your associates. Acting professionally is something which should be required by all who are involved with a business. Professionalism includes personal appearance, timeliness, manners, assistance and knowledge.

- The way that we think is usually evident in our appearance, business dealings, organizational skills, goals and personal demeanor. Your prevailing thoughts should be that you will be successful. Success with money will only be the end result of successful thinking, organizing, producing and marketing.

A P P E N D I X

SMALL BUSINESS ADMINISTRATION OFFICES

Alabama
District Office
2121 8th Ave. N.
Birmingham, AL
35203-2398
(205) 731-1344
Fax: (205) 731-1404

Alaska
District Office
222 W. 8th Ave.
Anchorage, AK
99513-7559
(907) 271-4022
Fax: (907) 271-4545

Arizona
District Office
2828 N. Central Ave.
Phoenix, AZ 85004-1025
(602) 640-2316
Fax: (602) 640-2360

Arkansas
District Office
2120 Riverfront Drive
Little Rock, AR 72202
(501) 324-5278
Fax: (501) 324-5199

California
District Office
2719 N. Air Fresno Dr.,
Suite 200
Fresno, CA 93727-1547

(209) 487-5791
Fax: (209) 487-5292

District Office
330 N. Brand Blvd.
Glendale, CA
91203-2304
(818) 552-3210
Fax: (818) 552-3260

District Office
660 J St., Suite 215
Sacramento, CA
95814-2413
(916) 498-6410
Fax: (916) 498-6422

District Office
550 W. C St.
San Diego, CA 92101
(619) 557-7252
Fax: (619) 557-5894

District Office
455 Market St., 6th Floor
San Francisco, CA
94105-2445
(415) 744-6820
Fax: (415) 744-6812

Regional Office
455 Market St., Suite 2200
San Francisco, CA 94105
(415) 744-2118
Fax: (415) 744-2119

District Office
200 W. Santa Ana Blvd.
#700

Santa Ana, CA 92701
(714) 550-7420
Fax: (714) 550-0191

Colorado
District Office
721 19th Street Suite 400
Denver, CO 80202
(303) 844-3984
Fax: (303) 844-6468

Regional Office
721 19th Street Suite 500
Denver, CO 80202
(303) 844-0500
Fax: (303) 844-0500

Connecticut
District Office
330 Main St.
Hartford, CT 06106
(203) 240-4700
Fax: (203) 240-4659

Delaware
Branch Office
824 N. Market St.
Wilmington, DE
19801-3011
(302) 573-6294
Fax: (302) 573-6060

District of Columbia
District Office
1110 Vermont Ave. NW
Washington, DC 20005

(202) 606-4000
Fax: (202) 606-4225

Florida
District Office
1320 S. Dixie Highway.
Coral Gables, FL
33146-2911
(305) 536-5521
Fax: (305) 536-5058

District Office
7825 Baymeadows Way
Jacksonville, FL
32256-7504
(904) 443-1900
Fax: (904) 443-1980

Georgia
District Office
1720 Peachtree Rd., NW
Atlanta, GA 30309-2482
(404) 347-4749
Fax: (404) 347-4745

Regional Office
1720 Peachtree Rd., NW
Atlanta, GA 30309-2482
(404) 347-4999
Fax: (404) 347-2355

Hawaii
District Office
300 Ala Moana Blvd.
Honolulu, HI 96850-4981
(808) 541-2990
Fax: (808) 541-2976

Idaho

District Office
1020 Main St.
Boise, ID 83702
(208) 334-1696
Fax: (208) 334-1696

Illinois

District Office
500 W. Madison St.
Chicago, IL 60661-2511
(312) 353-4528
Fax: (312) 886-5688

Regional Office
500 W. Madison St.
Chicago, IL 60661-2511
(312) 353-5000
Fax: (312) 353-3426

Branch Office
511 W. Capitol Ave.
Springfield, IL 62704
(217) 492-4416
Fax: (217) 492-4867

Indiana

District Office
429 N. Pennsylvania
Indianapolis, IN
    46204-1873
(317) 226-7272
Fax: (317) 226-7259

Iowa

District Office
215 4th Avenue Rd., SE
Cedar Rapids, IA
    52401-1806
(319) 362-6405
Fax: (319) 362-7861

District Office
210 Walnut St.
Des Moines, IA 50309
(515) 284-4422
Fax: (515) 284-4572

Kansas

District Office
100 E. English St.
Wichita, KS 67202
(316) 269-6616
Fax: (316) 269-6499

Kentucky

District Office
600 Dr. M.L. King Jr. Pl.
Louisville, KY 40202
(502) 582-5971
Fax: (502) 582-5009

Louisiana

District Office
365 Canal St.
New Orleans, LA 70130
(504) 589-6685
Fax: (504) 589-2339

Maine

District Office
40 Western Ave.
Augusta, ME 04330
(207) 622-8378
Fax: (207) 622-8277

Maryland

District Office
10 S. Howard St.
Baltimore, MD
    21201-2525
(410) 962-4392
Fax: (410) 962-1805

Massachusetts

District Office
10 Causeway St.
Boston, MA 02222-1093
(617) 565-5590
Fax: (617) 565-5598

Regional Office
10 Causeway St.
Boston, MA 02222-1093
(617) 565-8415
Fax: (617) 565-8420

Branch Office
1441 Main St., Suite 410
Springfield, MA 01103
(413) 785-0268
Fax: (413) 785-0267

Michigan

District Office
477 Michigan Ave.
Detroit, MI 48226
(313) 226-6075
Fax: (313) 226-4769

Branch Office
501 S. Front St.
Marquette, MI 49855
(906) 225-1108
Fax: (906) 225-1109

Minnesota

District Office
100 N. 6th St.
Minneapolis, MN
    55403-1563
(612) 370-2324
Fax: (612) 370-2303

Mississippi

Branch Office
One Bank of Mississippi
    Plaza, Suite 203
Gulfport, MS 39501-1949
(228) 863-4449
Fax: (228) 864-0179

District Office
101 W. Capitol St.
Jackson, MS 39201
(601) 965-4378
Fax: (601) 965-4294

Missouri

District Office
323 W. 8th. St., Suite 501
Kansas City, MO
    64105-1500
(816) 374-6708
Fax: (816) 374-6759

Regional Office
323 W. 8th St., Suite 307
Kansas City, MO
    64105-1500
(816) 374-6380
Fax: (816) 374-6339

Branch Office
620 S. Glenstone St.
Springfield, MO
    65802-3200
(417) 864-7670
Fax: (417) 864-4108

District Office
815 Olive St.
St. Louis, MO 63101
(314) 539-6600
Fax: (314) 539-3785

Montana

District Office
301 South Park
Helena, MT 59626
(406) 441-1081
Fax: (406) 441-1090

Nebraska

District Office
11145 Mill Valley Rd.
Omaha, NE 68154
(402) 221-4691
Fax: (402) 221-3680

Nevada

District Office
301 E. Stewart St.
Las Vegas, NV
    89125-2527
(702) 388-6611
Fax: (702) 388-6469

New Hampshire

District Office
143 N. Main St.
Concord, NH 03301
(603) 225-1400
Fax: (603) 225-1409

New Jersey

District Office
Two Gateway Center,
    4th Floor
Newark, NJ 07102
(973) 645-2434
Fax: (973) 645-6265

New Mexico

District Office
625 Silver Ave. SW
Albuquerque, NM 87102
(505) 766-1870
Fax: (505) 766-1057

New York

District Office
111 W. Huron St.
Buffalo, NY 14202
(716) 551-4301
Fax: (716) 551-4418

Branch Office
333 E. Water St.
Elmira, NY 14901
(607) 734-8130
Fax: (607) 733-4656

Branch Office
35 Pinelawn Rd.
Melville, NY 11747
(516) 454-0750
Fax: (516) 454-0769

District Office
26 Federal Plaza
New York, NY 10278
(212) 264-2454
Fax: (212) 264-7751

Regional Office
26 Federal Plaza
New York, NY 10278
(212) 264-1450
Fax: (212) 264-0038

Branch Office
100 State St.
Rochester, NY 14614
(716) 263-6700
Fax: (716) 263-3146

District Office
401 S. Salina St., 5th Floor
Syracuse, NY 13202
(315) 471-9393
Fax: (315) 471-9288

North Carolina

District Office
200 N. College St.
Charlotte, NC
    28202-2137
(704) 344-6563
Fax: (704) 344-6644

North Dakota

District Office
657 Second Ave. N.
Fargo, ND 58108
(701) 239-5131
Fax: (701) 239-5645

Ohio

Branch Office
525 Vine St.
Cincinnati, OH 45202
(513) 684-2814
Fax: (513) 684-3251

District Office
1111 Superior Ave.
Cleveland, OH
    44144-2507
(216) 522-4180
Fax: (216) 522-2038

District Office
2 Nationwide Plaza
Columbus, OH
    43215-2592
(614) 469-6860
Fax: (614) 469-2391

Oklahoma

District Office
210 Park Ave., Suite 1300
Oklahoma City, OK
    73102
(405) 231-5521
Fax: (405) 231-4876

Oregon

District Office
1515 S.W. Fifth Ave.
Portland, OR 97201-6695
(503) 326-2682
Fax: (503) 326-2808

Pennsylvania

Branch Office
100 Chestnut St.
Harrisburg, PA 17101
(717) 782-3840
Fax: (717) 782-4839

District Office
475 Allendale Rd.
King of Prussia, PA 19406
(610) 962-3800
Fax: (610) 962-3795

District Office
1000 Liberty Ave.,
    Federal Bldg.,
    Room 1128
Pittsburgh, PA
    15222-4004
(412) 395-6560
Fax: (412) 395-6562

Branch Office
20 N. Pennsylvania Ave.
Wilkes-Barre, PA
    18701-3589
(717) 826-6497
Fax: (717) 826-6287

Rhode Island

District Office
380 Westminister Mall
Providence, RI 02903
(401) 528-4562
Fax: (401) 528-4539

South Carolina

District Office
1835 Assembly St.
Columbia, SC 29201
(803) 765-5377
Fax: (803) 765-5962

South Dakota

District Office
101 S. Main Ave.
Sioux Falls, SD 57102
(605) 330-4231
Fax: (605) 330-4215

Tennessee

District Office
50 Vantage Way
Nashville, TN
    37228-1500
(615) 736-5881
Fax: (615) 736-7232

Texas

Branch Office
606 N. Carancahua
Corpus Christi, TX 78476
(512) 888-3331
Fax: (512) 888-3418

District Office
4300 Amon Carter Blvd.
Dallas/Ft.Worth, TX
    76155
(817) 885-6500
Fax: (817) 885-6516

Regional Office
4300 Amon Carter Blvd.
Dallas/Ft. Worth, TX
    76155
(817) 885-6581
Fax: (817) 885-6588

District Office
10737 Gateway W.
El Paso, TX 79935
(915) 540-5676
Fax: (915) 540-5636

District Office
222 E. Van Buren St.
Harlingen, TX 78550
(956) 427-8625
Fax: (956) 427-8537

District Office
9301 Southwest Freeway
Houston, TX 77074-1591
(713) 773-6500
Fax: (713) 773-6550

District Office
1611 Tenth St.
Lubbock, TX 79401-2693
(806) 472-7462
Fax: (806) 472-7487

District Office
727 E. Durango
San Antonio, TX 78206
(210) 472-5900
Fax: (210) 472-5937

Utah

District Office
125 S. State St.
Salt Lake City, UT 84138
(801) 524-5800
Fax: (801) 524-4160

Vermont

District Office
87 State St.
Montpelier, VT 05602
(802) 828-4422
Fax: (802) 828-4485

Virginia

District Office
1504 Santa Rosa Rd., Dale
   Bldg., Suite 200
Richmond, VA 23229
(804) 771-2400
Fax: (804) 771-8018

Washington

District Office
1200 Sixth Ave.,
   Suite 1700
Seattle, WA 98101-1128
(206) 553-7310
Fax: (206) 553-7099

Regional Office
1200 Sixth Ave.,
   Suite 1805
Seattle, WA 98101-1128
(206) 553-5676
Fax: (206) 553-2872

District Office
W. 601 First Ave.
Spokane, WA
   99204-0317
(509) 353-2800
Fax: (509) 353-2829

West Virginia

Branch Office
405 Capitol St., Suite 412
Charleston, WV 25301
(304) 347-5220
Fax: (304) 347-5350

District Office
168 W. Main St.
Clarksburg, WV 26301
(304) 623-5631
Fax: (304) 623-0023

Wisconsin

District Office
212 E. Washington Ave.
Madison, WI 53703
(608) 264-5261
Fax: (608) 264-5541

Branch Office
310 W. Wisconsin Ave.
Milwaukee, WI 53203
(414) 297-3941
Fax: (414) 297-1377

Wyoming

District Office
100 E. B St., Rm. 4001,
   Box 2839
Casper, WY 82602
(307) 261-6500
Fax: (307) 261-6535

Index